CHILDREN OF ABRAHAM

A REFORMED BAPTIST VIEW OF BAPTISM,
THE COVENANT, AND CHILDREN

And if ye be Christ's then are ye Abraham's seed,
and heirs according to the promise.

Henry E. Walter Ltd.
and
Carey Publications Ltd.

© Carey Publications Ltd.

ISBN 0 85479 7904

First printed 1973

Printed by
University Tutorial Press Ltd.
Foxton, near Cambridge, England
for
Henry E. Walter Ltd., 26 Grafton Road, Worthing
and
Carey Publications Ltd.
5 Fairford Close, Haywards Heath,
Sussex RH16 3EF.

TO GWYNETH

who lives Proverbs 31: 10-31

CONTENTS

Summary of Contents

Chapter 1. Baptism and the Covenant of Grace.

The argument for infant baptism based on covenant theology rests on four basic assertions.

1. God deals with his elect through a covenant.
2. The infants of believers are embraced with their believing parents in this covenant.
3. This applies to the New Testament era as well as the Old.
4. On this ground infants may be baptised.

The argument has strong appeal for the following reasons:

1. It seeks to provide a non-sacramental interpretation of infant baptism in opposition to the views of the Roman church.
2. It takes seriously the unity of the Bible, in which there is one covenant of grace only, embracing one church in both dispensations.
3. It seeks to provide a theology of children—an area in which Baptists have been weak.

If they are to meet this argument Baptists must do some hard theological thinking.

Chapter 2. Circumcision and Baptism.

The crux of the debate between Reformed Baptists and Paedobaptists is the analogy between baptism and circumcision. Paedobaptists argue that since the New Testament does not forbid infant baptism (is in fact silent on the matter), it should be practised on the same ground as circumcision in which, of course, children were included.

Karl Barth opposed this conclusion by suggesting that while circumcision had to do purely with natural membership of Israel as a nation, baptism had to do with spiritual membership of the church. But circumcision was also spiritual—a sign and seal of righteousness (Rom. 4: 11). It referred in typical form to the circumcision of the heart (Deut. 10: 16; Rom. 2: 29). It did have a national reference as well.

The analogy does in fact exist, but it is the nature of it which is in question. The covenant with Abraham included promises that his physical seed would be multiplied and given a land. In the New Testament this is seen as a spiritual seed and a spiritual inheritance. Thus circumcision signed and sealed the earthly things for all Jews, and the heavenly for believing Jews. Paedobaptists make the mistake of regarding the promises to the physical seed as being still in force. If this is so, believers must still be promised also the land of Canaan!

Circumcision is the type of which regeneration, not baptism, is the true antitype.

The abrogation of the principle "thee and thy seed" is seen in the New Covenant (Jer. 31: 31-34), where possession of inward spiritual life is required. Also in the baptism of John the Baptist there is no suggestion of infant seed being baptised, as paedobaptists admit. He therefore departed from the Old Covenant position and embraced the New with his demand for a new heart as the sign of Covenant membership.

Chapter 3. A Critique of Covenant Theology.

1. Covenant theologians apply the wrong method of exegesis. Instead of recognising that the New Testament fulfilment of the Covenant promises in Christ is far richer than the types of the Old Testament, they identify the two completely. Another weakness is the inferential argument that the silence of the New Testament as to a command to baptise infants is sufficient proof of the practice of infant baptism. Proselyte baptism also disproves, rather than proves, their case.

2. Paedobaptists are guilty of reading the Old Testament into the New. In the Old Testament, participation in the temporal, earthly blessings of the Covenant was sufficient to give a right to circumcision. Paedobaptists are, however, reluctant to admit this, as it would destroy the circumcision-baptism identity. Yet if they deny it, they then admit the necessity of faith. The attempt to prove from the disciplinary laws of Israel, that unbelievers were the

6

ones dealt with, is unreal. The delinquent was cut off as a breaker of the law, not as an unbeliever in the New Testament sense.

Embarrassment is also occasioned by the circumcision of Abraham's servants. Should servants today be baptised if they work in Christian households?

3. Many Paedobaptists read Old Testament into New and argue along the lines of national privilege. People born into Israel automatically inherited certain privileges. This shows their theocratic cast of mind. According to the New Testament, only those who share Abraham's faith are Abraham's seed (Gal. 3: 29).

Chapter 4. Towards a Baptist Theology of the Covenant.

The Covenant with Abraham looms large in the New Testament. Here we see that "his seed" are believers and believers only. Because of this there is no need for an express command forbidding the baptism of infants. The arguments from silence is from an empty not an eloquent silence.

The term seed is used in three senses referring to:—

1. Christ (Gal. 3: 16ff.).

2. Abraham's literal seed (John 8: 37, 39).

3. The true seed (Rom. 9: 7).

Paedobaptists, by saying that the children of the *flesh* are the children of God, are apparently unaware of 1 John 1: 12, 13.

Believers are spiritually circumcised as the seed of Abraham, and to them alone belongs baptism.

Far reaching implications flow from this position.

1. In respect of salvation. Reformed Baptists believe in Covenant grace which alone saves, and also in the necessity for repentance and faith.

2. In respect of the church. In the light of the New Covenant, the church membership should be composed as far as possible of true believers. We must work from this New Testament definition rather than from the existing situation. The 1689 Confession and all Reformed Baptists have refused to apply the parable of the wheat and tares to the church.

The historic Reformed Baptist position is one of strength, because it has a proper understanding of the relationship between

7

baptism and circumcision. It does justice to the continuity and diversity of revelation, it gives a proper view of family, church and state and it provides a ground for instruction of children. We do not assume that our children are regenerate.

Chapter 5. Children in the Old Testament.

Baptists have been re-examining the question of the relationship of children of believing parents to the church. Three aspects of the position of children in Old Testament Israel are considered.

1. Entry into the Covenant Community.

   Entry was by birth, and this was sealed by circumcision. Exclusion could be by death only, there was no provision for voluntary withdrawal. Paedobaptists who speak of the possibility of a child contracting out of the Covenant can find no support for this idea in the Old Testament.

2. Status within the Community.

   Children were not regarded as fully responsible adults until they were heads of households, they were, however, full members of Israel. No specific age of responsibility is suggested in Scripture. Children were subordinate and under instruction in the faith of Israel. We must recognise that not much is said on this subject in the Old Testament.

3. The Remnant: Election within Election.

   In Israel's later history the idea of the faithful remnant emerges. The remnant consisted of those who trembled at the Word. Children did not enter the remnant by birth, even if their parents were part of it, but by a spiritual change. We have in this a forerunner of the New Covenant. Hodge and others ignore the remnant idea and speak as if revelation on this matter ceased with Moses. The remnant shifts religion from a national basis to one in which the Covenant people must have a new heart. They must contract in!

Chapter 6. Children in the New Testament.

John the Baptist clearly challenges the reliance of the Jews upon their physical descent from Abraham. He did not regard membership of the Messianic community as being determined by birth into Israel. Both Christ and Paul stress the same thing, yet today many still believe that all infant seed are children of promise. This leads to carnal security.

1. Children in the teaching of our Lord.

   Two passages are important (Matt. 18: 1-6 and 19: 13-15). In the first he teaches that unless men become insignificant, like children in the ancient world, they cannot be converted. Jesus is not teaching that children have spiritual qualities like humility, neither is he teaching that all children, as children, are in the Kingdom. Christ speaks here of the little ones who believe in him, a phrase which can include adults, and which implies that not all children believe. In the second passage in Matthew, the phrase "of such is the kingdom of heaven" does not mean that only children are in the kingdom. It means that the kingdom belongs to the childlike, including in this group some children. This says nothing of "Covenant" children, and if used to justify infant baptism would justify the baptism of all children.

2. Children in the rest of the New Testament.

   Acts 2: 29 provides no warrant for infant baptism as Alford claims.

   1 Cor. 7: 14 according to our Paedobaptist friends positively gushes the water of baptism! The problem is that if the children are holy and to be baptised, so is the unbelieving partner. The same word is used for both.

Chapter 7. Children and Regeneration.

Little biblical teaching is found on this subject. Problems concerning repentance and faith, and responsibility in young children arise.

1. Children and their Adamic status.

   All children are born in Adam, and thus in sin. They require regeneration before they can be in Christ (John 3: 6, 7; 1 Cor. 15: 50).

2. Children and the grace of God.

   Children are not saved because of supposed innocence. This denies the grace of God. Apart from free grace they are eternally lost. Nor are they safe until the age of discretion. The Bible nowhere defines such an age.

But can children repent and believe? It is dangerous to stress too much their psychological inability to believe for adults, too, are psychologically unable to believe and the natural man does not receive the things of the Spirit. Faith can be given by grace to children as to adults.

3. Infant Salvation.

The Scriptures do not expressly state that all children dying in infancy are saved. God may in fact save all such, as he certainly can, but he has not told us whether he does or not. Though children of believers are not Christian children, nor members of the church, they have great privileges. Yet we must treat them as unconverted until there is evidence of a saving change. This was the approach of our Lord, when he said to one Covenant child, still contracted in: "Ye must be born again".

Definition of Terms

Some readers may not be accustomed to the terms used by theologians and may wonder why it is necessary to use such terms as "polemical" and "hermeneutics". Such terms are useful, provided that their meaning is clearly understood. They have the advantage of reducing the number of words which would otherwise have to be used!

Polemic means of or pertaining to controversy. Our Lord, for example, engaged in controversy with the Jews. In the more restricted sense the noun is applied to theological disputation. Polemic then is the basis from which we reason a case. It is easier to use one word in such instances.

Hermeneutics is the science of interpretation. Scripture, like any other literature, must be properly interpreted by employing clearly defined principles. Scriptural hermeneutics takes into account, for example, the various types of literature found in the Bible, such as history, poetry, prophecy and seeks to interpret them in accordance with their differing characteristics.

Apologetics is another word which theologians use that is not always understood. It means the way in which we argue, reason or explain in defence of the faith; it would be wrong to apologise for the faith, for we should be so certain of it as never to be sorry about any part of it.

Exegesis is another term frequently used. It means the drawing or extracting from the actual text of Scripture in a careful way its correct meaning. Exposition implies the same thing but is a more general term which covers also the application of the meaning of the text to either readers or hearers. In Chapter 6 of this book you have an example of careful exegesis. The need for this is inescapable. If people build a theory on the false foundation of erroneous exegesis there is no alternative but to disentangle the details. In order that the exegesis may be followed by those without a knowledge of Greek, we have translated Greek words into English.

Our desire is that all God's people should know and experience as much of his Word as possible. We would be sorry if believers were put off because of terminology which, though it may not seem to be the case at first, actually enables writers to use less words and employ shorter sentences.

Introduction

I have written this book because I hold certain, strong convictions. The first is that it is worse than useless to pretend there are no real differences between Calvinistic Baptists, of whom I am one, and their Calvinistic brethren who practise infant baptism. These differences—over the doctrine of the church, and the subjects and mode of baptism—are important because they involve matters about which Scripture speaks, I believe, very clearly. Today in many quarters I find that they are dismissed rather lightly in the interests of bringing about a closer degree of unity between Calvinistic churches. Whilst I abhor controversy for controversy's sake, I cannot feel that the cause of Christ is well served by what I can only call "the lowest common denominator" approach to the whole issue of unity.

My second conviction is that both non-Calvinistic Baptists and Calvinistic Paedobaptists need to become aware that there is a case for believers' baptism which seeks to do justice to both the unity and diversity of God's gracious covenant, which has found expression in various historical covenants recorded in Holy Scripture. Too often, even in this day and age, are "Anabaptist" and "Reformed" put in opposition, as if there had never existed a consistent stream of Reformed Baptist theology which has maintained believers' baptism on a Calvinistic basis. Furthermore, it is time that non-Calvinistic Baptists, who form the majority in the worldwide Baptist movement, were brought to realise that one can be a Calvinist and remain a Baptist! More than once I have been told that one cannot be both.

Thirdly, I believe that the doctrine of the "gathered" church, must be maintained "come wind, come weather". By "gathered" church I mean that visible, local churches are to be, so far as is possible, composed of "visible saints" who give clear evidence of having been regenerated by the Holy Spirit and called by grace. The church of Christ was never meant to be a field of wheat and tares, but a community "sanctified in Christ Jesus, called to be saints" (1 Cor. 1: 2). Had this truth been maintained throughout

Christian history, many problems which face us today would never have been created.

Lastly, I am sure that for Baptists merely to reject infant baptism is not enough. They must give attention to the theology of children in general and to that of believers' children in particular. I have tried, therefore, in the second part of the book, to grapple with some of the issues raised by the position of children in homes where infant baptism is rejected.

The substance of Part One was first given in September, 1968, at the annual Summer School in Theology of the Irish Baptist College, Belfast, and later at the first Carey Conference which was held at Wadderton, near Birmingham, in January, 1970. Chapter Two was given also a special lecture at Central Baptist Church, Pretoria, Republic of South Africa, in March, 1971, and to the Border Baptist Association Ministers' Fraternal at East London in the same month. Part Two consists of papers given at the second Carey Conference held at Nottingham in July, 1972.

My sincere thanks are due to my secretary, Mrs. Constance Black, who with painstaking care has produce an accurate typescript from a rather illegible longhand. Various friends have read the manuscript and made valuable comments. The Reverend John Legg, of Northallerton, has brought his keenly critical mind to bear upon my thinking. His comments have been all the more helpful as he is a Reformed Paedobaptist. Dr. Edmund Jonker, of Lynnwood Glen, Pretoria, not only read the manuscript but suggested the title. Dr. Robin Wells, of Sandton, Transvaal, subjected my work to keen critical scrutiny. Herbert Carson, minister of Hamilton Road Baptist Church, Bangor, N. Ireland, looked at my work from the standpoint of a former Anglican who once argued for infant baptism on the basis of covenant theology. Erroll Hulse, the pastor of Cuckfield Baptist Church, Sussex, has played the part of an exhorter, spurring me on to complete the task of writing when other duties threatened to delay its appearance unduly. Needless to say, I alone am responsible for the views expressed.

Without the constant support of my wife, Gwyneth, this book could not have been written. It is fitting, therefore, that it should be dedicated to her.

THE IRISH BAPTIST COLLEGE,
BELFAST.
September, 1972.

14

CHAPTER 1

BAPTISM AND THE COVENANT OF GRACE

In this chapter I want to examine what is meant by the term "covenant theology" as it is understood by our Reformed Paedobaptist brethren. Unless we are clear about what they understand by covenant theology we shall not appreciate why they are so sure that the practice of baptising the infants of believers has Scriptural warrant. Furthermore, it is important that we realise that covenant theology involves, as we shall see, a certain understanding of the relationship between the Old and New Testaments. This matter I believe to be a key issue in the debate between us. We should also be aware of the type of inferential reasoning (to be examined later) which is employed by Reformed theologians to establish the Paedobaptist case.

Assertions of Covenant Theology

To illustrate what is meant by covenant theology in general and the argument for infant baptism which is based upon it, I can, I think, do no better than quote a statement by Professor John Murray. He writes:

"The argument for infant baptism rests upon the recognition that God's redemptive action and revelation in this world are covenantal; in a word, redemptive action is covenant action, and redemptive revelation is covenant revelation. Embedded in this covenantal action of God is the principle that the infant seed of believers are embraced with their parents in the covenant relation and provision. It is this method of God's administration of grace in the world that must be appreciated; it belongs to the New Testament as well as to the Old. It is its presence and significance that grounds infant baptism; and it is the perception of its significance that illuminates for us the meaning of this ordinance." [1]

Now if we analyse his statement we find that he makes several very important theological assertions.

Firstly, he says that God deals with that people whom he purposes to redeem on the basis of covenant; that is, in his sovereign grace he binds himself to save his church, by declaring and manifesting himself to be their God (Gen. 17: 7). On their part, his people take upon themselves the obligation, as vassals of the only Potentate and King of kings, of covenant loyalty, that is, the obligation to render homage, worship, obedience and service to Almighty God. The covenant demands that go with the revelation of covenant grace are summed up in the command which immediately follows God's identification of himself to Abraham as the Almighty God—"Walk before me and be thou perfect!" (Gen. 17: 1). It is not, of course, man's promising obedience to God that constrains God's favour to man, since there can be no question here of a covenant between equals, or of sinful man offering his service to God in order to obtain God's favour; rather, it is the manifestation of grace which, as the New Testament clearly shows, calls forth the loving obedience of those who enjoy the blessings of the covenant (*e.g.* Rom. 12: 1).

Secondly, Professor Murray states that the infant seed c believers are embraced with their parents in the covenant relatio and provisions. In other words, the blessings of the covenant are promised not to believing adults only, but to their children who do not yet believe, yet who are none the less included within the covenant along with their parents. The classical proof of this belief is found in Gen. 17: 7-10, with its repeated emphasis on "thee and thy seed". Reformed Paedobaptists would claim the operation throughout the Old Testament of the principle that to believers and their seed are promised the blessings of the covenant.

Thirdly, Professor Murray also states that the principle that the infant seed of believers are embraced with their parents in the covenant relation and provision is not set aside in the present dispensation [*i.e.* the "last days" (Heb. 1: 2) in which we live] which has been inaugurated by the advent and redemptive ministry of the Messiah. Rather it is carried over from the Old into the New Dispensation. "It belongs," he says, "to the New as well as to the Old."

Fourthly, it is this principle which supplies the *raison d'être* for the practice of infant baptism and gives it its meaning. The argument as it is usually put runs like this: since in the Abrahamic covenant the covenant sign of circumcision was applied to his seed, baptism which is one sign of the New covenant (the Lord's Supper being the other) ought to be given to the infant-seed of believers. In the same way that circumcision was given in the Old dispensation to the infant seed of believers, baptism which has come in the place of circumcision ought to be given to the infant seed of believers in the New.

Baptist Reaction

Now the reaction of many present-day Baptists to the type of reasoning expounded here is to dismiss it very simply in one sentence as "Old Testament" teaching. The assumption is that it has no relevance to the New Testament. When confronted by the analogy between circumcision and baptism they deny that there is any connection whatsoever between the two ordinances; the one, they say, is Old Testament, the other New Testament. Yet they do not dismiss the analogy between the Passover and the Lord's Supper in the same way. Now such a reaction on the part of a non-Reformed Baptists is calculated to earn the scorn of any well-instructed Paedobaptist of the Reformed tradition, and rightly so! He will point out to Baptists who argue in this way that the view of the Old Testament which they espouse is as old as Marcion, the second century heretic, who, thinking to exalt the superiority of the New, dismissed the Old Testament as Jewish and inferior. But if one writes off the Old Testament in such a fashion what then becomes of the unity of the Bible? How could the apostle Paul have argued, as he does, that the Abrahamic Covenant was not only not disannulled by the Mosaic, but is operative now (Gal. 3: 14-29, especially vv. 17 and 29)? How could Peter declare, "Ye are the children of the prophets and of the covenant which God made with our fathers saying unto Abraham, 'And in thy seed shall all the kindreds of the earth be blessed' " (Acts 3: 25)? Those who so sharply distinguish between the Old Testament and the New are at a loss, I suggest, to explain these statements and many more which presuppose a basic unity between the two Testaments. However, present day non-Reformed Baptists and Reformed Paedobaptists need to become aware of the fact that, historically speaking, there is a powerful stream of Baptist apologetic which, while it issues from Reformed theology, exposes the weaknesses of the covenantal argument for infant baptism. Thomas Patient in his pamphlet *The Doctrine of Baptism and the Distinction of the Covenants* (1654) was one of the first Particular (Calvinistic) Baptists to attempt a rebuttal of Paedobaptism. Patient has been followed by a notable succession of Calvinistic Baptists who have accepted covenant theology without losing their hold on believers' baptism in any way. The names of John Bunyan, John Gill, Abraham Booth, Alexander Carson and C. H. Spurgeon are representative of a Particular Baptist tradition which is consistent with covenant theology.

If we are to understand the continuing appeal of the case for infant baptism based on covenant theology, we must take note of the following points and reckon seriously with them.

A Non-Sacramental View of Infant Baptism

Firstly, *covenant theologians have put forward a non-sacramental interpretation of infant baptism*, in contrast to Anglo-Catholicism and Lutheranism. The Reformers answered the medieval Roman Catholic doctrine of "ex opere operato", according to which the blessings of regeneration and remission of sin were tied to infant baptism, by asserting the principle "nullum sacramentum sine fide", that is, where faith is not to be found there is no sacrament. This principle might, at first sight, appear to concede the case to Baptists who have always insisted that faith in Christ as Saviour should precede baptism, but in fact Reformed theologians have generally held that faith may either precede, coincide with, or follow baptism. They have emphasised that the above-mentioned principle is not to be understood as requiring that faith must be operative in the recipient prior to baptism; rather, it is urged that the benefits of the sacrament of baptism are appropriated through faith without regard to any necessity that faith should precede baptism.

Baptists have not always understood that the position held by these Reformers was worked out in antithesis to the view of Rome. They have, therefore, failed to appreciate that the Reformers were not labouring to establish the Baptist position, that faith should come before baptism, but rather they were endeavouring to express a non-sacramental view of the Lord's supper and baptism. Zwingli, who is one of the key figures in the history of covenant theology (indeed he might be called the father of it), was well aware that his reasoning marked a radical departure from the theology of the

18

medieval Roman Catholic Church. He stated: "In this matter of baptism, if I may be pardoned for saying it, *I can only conclude that all the doctors have been in error from the times of the Apostles.* This is a serious and weighty assertion, and I make it with such reluctance, that had I not been compelled to do so by contentious spirits (*i.e.* by the Zurich Anabaptists) I would have preferred to keep silence, and simply teach the truth. But it will be seen that the assertion is a true one, for all the doctors have ascribed to the water a power it did not have, and the holy apostles did not teach. They have also misunderstood the saying of Christ on water and the Holy Ghost in John 3. Our present task is to see what baptism really is. *At many points we shall have to tread a different path from that taken by either ancient or more modern writers or by our own contemporaries. We shall not be guided by our own caprice, but by the Word of God."* [2]

Zwingli had to fight, as I have already implied, on two fronts; on the one hand he had to oppose the Roman view of baptism as necessary to salvation, and on the other hand he wanted to maintain the practice of infant baptism against the attacks and objections of the Anabaptists. In short, Zwingli was under the necessity of advancing a case for infant baptism based upon a non-sacramental view of the rite, whilst at the same time attempting to provide for it an adequate biblical basis. Since Zwingli's time his arguments have been refined, but the motive has never been changed, namely, the desire for a biblical, non-sacramental foundation for infant baptism, which will be in harmony with the evangelicalism of the Reformation.

Now, while it may be true that some Reformed theologians have exhibited a tendency to move in the direction of the Roman doctrine of baptism, it will not do for fervent Baptists to assume that the practice of infant baptism inevitably requires a belief in baptismal regeneration. In my opinion Klaas Runia's statement cannot be controverted: "In Reformed theology there is no place for baptismal regeneration in the proper sense of the word. Fully acknowledging the sacraments as primarily divine acts, it nevertheless rejects any idea of an infusion of grace, *i.e.* regeneration, by the sacraments themselves. There is no inclusion of grace in the sacraments or amalgamation between the sign and the matter signified, so that the sacraments may be seen as channels of grace." [3]

I have spent some time on this point because Baptists must

appreciate that Reformed Paedobaptists are not simply being perversely blind in the face of undeniable evidence in favour of believers' baptism. Unless they do appreciate this, they will not take covenant theology seriously, as the only possible alternative to the Baptist position which will comply with the basic evangelicalism of both Baptist and Reformed traditions. Present day Baptists will do well to heed and indeed ponder Jewett's judgment: "The theological conception sometimes called covenant theology which undergirds the Paedobaptist argument at this point, is too grand, too challenging, too persistent to be ignored with impunity. The dogmatician who slights it despises his own reputation. This is perhaps to concede that the Baptists as a whole have not been outstanding theologians; the stream of their rebuttal has run so thin at this juncture that only the hollow eyes of predisposition could fail to see its inadequacy and judge the counter arguments superior." [4]

The Unity of the Bible

The second reason why the argument for infant baptism based on covenant theology continues to make such a strong appeal is because *it takes seriously the unity of the Bible*. Its starting point is that there is one covenant of grace which has been operative in human history since the Fall, the substance of which is the divine promise made to elect sinners, "I will be your God and you shall be my people". From the first disclosure of grace in the "protevangelium" (Gen. 3: 15), to the final vision of John the apostle, "Behold the tabernacle of God is with men, and he will dwell with them, and be their God" (Rev. 21: 3), Holy Scripture shows that there is but one covenant of grace throughout all ages. From the unity of the covenant certain conclusions follow:

(a) There is one Church of God, purchased with the blood of Christ, which embraces the people of God in all ages and in all places.

(b) There is one way of salvation, namely, repentance toward God and faith in our Lord Jesus Christ, the mediator of the eternal covenant.

(c) There is one destiny of the saints, Mount Zion, the Heavenly City, the new Jerusalem.

A great deal of Baptist apologetic, so it seems to me, has failed to come to terms with the indubitable fact that the covenant of

20

grace, although it exhibits diversity of administration in the time of promise and in the time of fulfilment, is none-the-less one covenant. As we shall see in a subsequent chapter, Reformed Paedobaptists argue from this fact to a wrong conclusion, namely, that as children were circumcised under the old economy, so they ought to be baptised under the new. Nevertheless their basic contention is correct—the covenant of grace is one in all ages. In my view Baptists will never seriously disturb Reformed Paedobaptists until they see this. The divisive, atomistic approach of so much contemporary Baptist apologetic is about as effective at this point as a shot-gun against a Sherman tank.

Theology of Believers' Children

Another reason why the covenant argument for infant baptism continues to be so appealing is that it seeks to *provide a theology of believers' children*—and perhaps, after all, this is its chief appeal. It must be admitted that Baptists generally have given little thought to this matter. Whilst I dissent very strongly from some of the conclusions of the report published by the Baptist Union of Great Britain and Ireland entitled, *The Child and the Church* (1966), I think that the thrust of the following quotation cannot be denied. "Baptists have rejected infant baptism without facing the problems created by the rejection of it. We have upheld believers' baptism, the necessity of conversion and the concept of a regenerate Church without apparently realising that all these great truths do not answer all the questions which confront men in the life of the people of God. Even when members of Paedobaptist communions feel the force and attractiveness of the case for believers' baptism they still feel that Baptists leave unanswered important questions concerning children. We can scarcely deny that this is true. The conversion theology which dominates Baptist doctrines of baptism and of the Church is, in itself, silent about the infant; it looks forward to the time of his response to Christ, but on his present state it does not speak. But what if he does not live to the age of response, what is the status of those who have not had opportunity to believe and who are therefore not dealt with by this conversion theology? For the sake of the denomination as well as its testimony to others, Baptists need to look at such questions."[5] Although I find myself unable to agree with the answers given in the report, I think its authors are, at least, asking the right questions.

For three main reasons then, the argument for infant baptism which is grounded in covenant theology continues to exercise a very real attraction in Reformed circles. Firstly, it provides a non-sacramental rationale for the practice of infant baptism. Secondly, it regards with utmost seriousness the unity of the covenant. Thirdly, it seems to provide a theology for believers' children. If the far-reaching challenge of the Reformed Paedobaptist position is to be met, Reformed Baptists must do some hard theological thinking. In particular they must consider the following matters. Firstly, the relationship between the administration of the covenant of grace under the old economy and under the new. Secondly, they must address themselves to the question of the undoubted analogy between circumcision and baptism, and they must inquire as to the exact significance of that analogy. Thirdly, they must give attention to the position of believers' children.

NOTES

1. John Murray, *Christian Baptism,* Presbyterian and Reformed, Philadelphia, 1962, p. 2.
2. Ulrich Zwingli, *Of Baptism*, p. 130, quoted by Paul King Jewett, *Infant Baptism and Confirmation,* 1960, p. 143 (his italics). This valuable work in mimeographed form may be obtained from Fuller Theological Seminary, Pasadena, California, U.S.A.
3. Article "Baptismal Regeneration" in *Encyclopaedia of Christianity*, The National Foundation for Christian Education, Wilmington, U.S.A., 1964, Vol. 1. p. 541.
4. Paul King Jewett, article "Baptism (Baptist View)", *Encyclopaedia of Christianity,* Vol. 1. p. 524.
5. *The Child and the Church*, Baptist Union of Great Britain and Ireland, London, 1966.

CHAPTER 2

CIRCUMCISION AND BAPTISM

We come now to the main point of the difference between Reformed Baptists and Reformed Paedobaptists. Central to covenant theology, as employed to provide a basis for infant baptism, is the analogy between circumcision and baptism. This analogy had been noticed and employed centuries before the Reformation, although it had never been central to the argument for infant baptism. One finds this analogy noticed by Augustine, but he made little use of it. However, when the Reformers wanted to retain the practice of infant baptism in the Reformed churches against the Anabaptist challenge, the analogy between circumcision and baptism was brought to the forefront of the debate, and there it has remained ever since as far as Reformed Paedobaptists are concerned.

We may appreciate the use to which the circumcision-baptism analogy is put by looking at the Heidelberg Catechism (1563), which is of the highest authority in Dutch and German Reformed circles. Question 74 asks, "Are infants also to be baptised?" To this question the answer is given, "Yes, for since they, as well as the adult, are included in the covenant and church of God; and since redemption from sin by the blood of Christ, and the Holy Ghost, the author of faith, is promised to them no less than to the adult; they must, therefore, by baptism, as a sign of the covenant, be also admitted into the christian church; and be distinguished from the children of infidels, as was done in the old covenant, or testament, by circumcision, instead of which, baptism is instituted in the new covenant". The argument, which is really in the form of a syllogism, is clear and straightforward:

(1) The covenant of grace belongs not to believers only, but also to their children.

(2) The covenant sign in the Old Testament was circumcision, which was applied to children, as well as in certain cases to adults.

23

(3) The covenant sign in the New Testament is baptism, which has replaced circumcision and should be applied to both believers *and* their children.

In Reformed Paedobaptist apologetic the circumcision-baptism analogy is employed as a hammer against the advocates of believers' baptism in a way which, to the unwary, has a peculiarly compelling force. One can almost sense Professor Murray's elation as he throws out the following challenge to Baptists:

"We come now," says the Professor, "to the question which cannot be suppressed or evaded, and which cannot be pressed with too much emphasis. If children born of the faithful were given the sign and seal of the covenant, and therefore the richest blessings which the covenant disclosed, if the New Testament economy is the elaboration and extension of this covenant of which circumcision was the sign, are we to believe that infants in this age are excluded from that which was provided by the Abrahamic covenant? In other words, are we to believe that infants may not properly be given the sign of that blessing which is enshrined in the new covenant? Is the new covenant in this respect less generous than was the Abrahamic? Is there less efficacy, as far as infants are concerned, in the new covenant than there was in the old? Are infants in the new dispensation more inhabile to the grace of God? These are questions that cannot be lightly dismissed." [1]

Professor Murray's series of interrogatives rests, it is apparent, on what he regards as so compelling an inference from the Abrahamic covenant, that an express New Testament warrant to baptise infants is not only not to be demanded, but is *not* in the nature of the case to be expected! There is not, he would argue, a hint of the revocation of the principle that infants are included in the covenant along with their believing parents. Therefore the silence of the New Testament proves that the principle of the covenant membership of children of believers is still in force. Not only so, an express New Testament warrant for the baptism of infants is unnecessary, since it would have been understood by every Jew in the New Testament era that the Abrahamic covenant still held good. For Professor Murray and other Reformed Paedobaptist theologians the very silence of the New Testament as to the baptism of infants, far from appearing as a weakness, is claimed as a strength.

24

The silence of the New Testament as to the practice of the baptism of infants is claimed as supporting the practice of it in the Apostolic Church. "In reality," writes Pierre Charles Marcel, "the silence of the New Testament regarding the baptism of infants militates in favour of, rather than against, this practice. To overthrow completely notions so vital, pressed for more than two thousand years on the soul of the people, to withdraw from children the sacrament of admission into the covenant, the Apostolic Church ought to have received from the Lord *an explicit prohibition*, so revolutionary in itself, that a record of it would have been preserved in the New Testament." [2]

In such a fashion the Baptist type of proof-text method, which argues from the silence of the New Testament *against* infant baptism, is countered. Certainly one must candidly admit that if Baptists rely on the argument from silence *alone*, they will get, inevitably, the worst of the argument, since it is an undoubted fact that male children were included in the Abrahamic covenant, and were accordingly circumcised.

Karl Barth's Dichotomy

One way of attempting to meet the challenge of the Paedobaptist argument is to posit an extreme dichotomy, a complete distinction between circumcision and baptism. This is basically the method of Karl Barth in his famous pamphlet that rocked the theological world on the Continent of Europe.[3] Barth denies that baptism should be administered to infants on the following grounds.

Though baptism has come in the place of circumcision it may not be administered to the children of believers, because circumcision deals with the natural, *i.e.* the sacred lineage that reached its end in the coming of the Messiah, who was the seed of David. Circumcision is pre-messianic and is tied to the natural lineage, but with the advent of the Kingdom of God in the person and work of the Messiah, not natural but spiritual birth is required of those who would enjoy the blessings of salvation. By Barth's construction then, circumcision is the sign appropriate to natural birth into the covenant people of Israel, whereas baptism has to do with that birth by the Spirit which alone brings a man into the Kingdom of God.

The very neatness of Barth's construction makes it superficially attractive, but it will not, I believe, stand up to sustained and serious theological scrutiny for three reasons. Firstly, the New Testament itself will not permit us to say that circumcision had a purely natural reference. According to Rom. 4: 11, "Abraham received the sign of circumcision, a seal of the righteousness by faith, which he had yet being uncircumcised". A sign which had a purely natural reference could hardly be the sign and seal of justification by faith through grace. Circumcision therefore has a spiritual significance which will not allow us to restrict its meaning the way Barth does.

Secondly, although circumcision was performed on the organ of generation, as a rite it referred typically to the necessity of the circumcision of the heart. This demand for the circumcision of the heart is made throughout the Old Testament and it is especially prominent in the prophetic literature. Deut. 10: 16 is an instructive example. It says, "Circumcise therefore the foreskin of your heart and be no more stiffnecked". This is a call for obedience to "the Lord your God, for he is God of gods and Lord of lords, a great God, a mighty and a terrible" (v. 17). Deut. 30: 6 is also important, "And the Lord thy God will circumcise thy heart and the heart of thy seed, to love the Lord thy God with all thy heart and with all thy soul, that thou mayest live". So it is through the circumcision of the heart that a man is enabled to love the Lord his God and give obedience to him. Jer. 4. 4 is notable: "Circumcise yourselves to the Lord and take away the foreskin of your hearts, ye men of Judah and inhabitants of Jerusalem, lest my fury come forth like fire to burn that none can quench it, because of the evil of your doings". Here the call to repentance is issued under the figure of the circumcision of the heart. The following New Testament references are particularly relevant: "But he is a Jew who is one inwardly and whose circumcision is of the heart, in the Spirit and not in the letter, whose praise is not of men but of God" (Rom. 2: 29). "For we are the circumcision which worship God in the Spirit and rejoice in Christ Jesus, and have no confidence in the flesh" (Phil. 3: 3), *i.e.* they put no confidence in mere outward circumcision, but rejoice in the fact that they are regenerate through the grace of God and thus are circumcised in heart. So, circumcision as a rite refers to the necessity of the circumcision of the heart, and therefore it cannot be said to have an exclusively natural reference.

Thirdly, to be uncircumcised in heart is to be in a state of spiritual and moral uncleanness. Thus we read in Exod. 6: 12 of

26

"uncircumcised lips", *i.e.* unclean lips; in Lev. 19: 23 of "uncircumcised fruit", *i.e.* fruit which for three years must be regarded as unclean and unfit for eating; in Acts 7: 51 of "stiffnecked people, uncircumcised in heart and ears". Such persons are in a state of moral and spiritual blindness, resisting the Holy Spirit. So Barth's dichotomy, his sharp division between "carnal" circumcision and "spiritual" baptism, is not in my opinion warranted by Scripture. The solution to the problem of the relation between circumcision and baptism will have to be sought elsewhere.

Circumcision—A National Sign

Another way of attempting to meet the challenge posed by the circumcision-baptism analogy is to interpret circumcision as a purely national sign, whereas baptism is viewed as the initiatory ordinance of the Church. Now, whilst it is true that circumcision did mark off Israel as a nation from the nations round about her (thus the Philistines could be described as the uncircumcised), it cannot be said that circumcision had the purely national reference which this antithesis would presuppose. That this is so can be seen from the fact that circumcision was not introduced as the covenant sign at Sinai, when the nation pledged itself to keep God's law and to obey his covenant. This we see if we consult Exod. 19: 5, 6, 8. "Now therefore if ye will obey my voice indeed and keep my covenant, then shall ye be unto me a peculiar treasure above all people, for all the earth is mine; And Moses came and called for the elders of the people, and laid before their faces all these words which the Lord commanded him. And all the people answered together, and said, All that the Lord hath spoken we will do. And Moses returned the words of the people unto the Lord."

Circumcision, although it was taken up into the Mosaic law and included within it, was initially bestowed not upon Moses but upon Abraham (see Gen. 17). In other words, as the sign of God's covenant with Abraham, circumcision was imposed, as Paul says, 430 years before the giving of the law to the nation in the Sinaitic covenant (Gal. 3: 17). Circumcision then must not be viewed as belonging only to the national, legal and theocratic stage of Israel's history, in contrast to baptism which pertains to the new covenant, which is not in the letter but of the Spirit (2 Cor. 3: 6). Circumcision was enjoined on Abraham and his family before ever Israel became a nation. It was not a legal ordinance, but the sign in

27

Abraham's flesh of God's gracious covenant with him and with his seed. Now if we accept this, as the evidence surely compels us to do, then we cannot interpret circumcision as a sign only of Israel's national separation to God. It was this of course, but its significance as a sign is not exhausted by describing it as a merely national sign. Whilst it was taken up into the Mosaic covenant it preceded it as the covenant sign by many generations, and thus it cannot be interpreted exclusively as a national sign.

It is my considered opinion that Baptists must recognise the analogy between circumcision and baptism. It seems to me pointless to deny the existence of this analogy, yet it is often done. One appreciates why there has been a marked reluctance to recognise its existence, namely, because of the fear that to recognise the analogy would mean the opening of the door to the practice of infant baptism since, as circumcision was applied to Abraham and his seed, baptism should be applied to believers and their seed. To illustrate this point, I have been told more than once, that if you embrace covenant theology you cannot really be a Baptist. However, as I shall argue later, such a consequence need not, indeed should not, follow upon a recognition of the analogy between circumcision and baptism. The crucial issue is, to my mind, not that there is an analogy but rather the nature of the analogy that exists! As we shall see, Reformed Paedobaptists frequently make circumcision, for all practical purposes, identical in meaning to baptism. James Bannerman, for example, states that whatever you can say about circumcision you can say about baptism, because their meaning is identical.[4] It is this identity of meaning to which I object, but not the analogy itself.

The Analogy

Having stated that I personally accept that there is an analogy I must give my reasons for doing so. Firstly, circumcision in the Old Testament is a symbol of renewal and cleansing of the heart. As we have seen already, a circumcised heart is a heart enabled by God to receive spiritual truths and submit to the divine will (Deut. 10: 16; 30: 6; Jer. 4: 4; 9: 26; Ezek. 44: 7). An uncircumcised heart, on the other hand, exhibits a lack of receptivity to the divine commands. Now it can hardly be denied that baptism in the New Testament has much the same meaning and import. In Col. 2: 11 whether we take the phrase "the circumcision of Christ" as having

28

an objective meaning, *i.e.* the cross, or whether we take it subjectively to mean the spiritual and moral renewal of the believer in regeneration, the analogy between circumcision in its spiritual sense and baptism seems patently clear.[5] Paul is here asserting that those who are "in Christ" (v. 10) have been inwardly circumcised, with a circumcision "not made with hands". In this circumcision the believer has put off the body of the flesh ("of the sins" is not in the best manuscripts), language which at once puts us into a baptismal context. "Putting off" one's past existence dominated by sin, and "putting on Christ", are connected with baptism and its significance. For example, according to Rom. 6: 6 believers declare that in baptism the body of sin has been destroyed. Furthermore, Paul states in Gal. 3: 27 that "as many of you as have been baptised into Christ have put on Christ". In the light of such expressions, "putting off the flesh", "putting on Christ", it is plain that baptism is close in meaning to the *symbolic* significance of circumcision. Moreover, the continued use of the aorist passive in Col. 2: 11 ff. makes it clear that, as Jewett says, "to experience the circumcision of Christ in the putting off of the body of the flesh, is the same as being buried with him and raised with him in baptism through faith. If this be so, the only conclusion we can reach is that the two signs as outward rites symbolise the same inner reality in Paul's thinking. So circumcision may fairly be said to be the Old Testament counterpart of Christian baptism".[6] A further piece of evidence is that the language of Rom. 4: 11, describing Abraham's circumcision as the sign and seal of the righteousness that is by faith, which he had before being circumcised, could be equally well applied to baptism.

Having then, I trust, justified my assertion that there is an analogy existing between circumcision and baptism, we must now enquire into the precise meaning and significance of that analogy. This we shall do, firstly, by studying the institution of circumcision in Gen. 17, and secondly, by examining the New Testament interpretation of the rite of circumcision.

Institution of Circumcision

It is evident on examination of Genesis 17 that the covenant with Abraham had both dispensational and trans-dispensational elements. In other words, the promised blessings of the covenant were implemented, either in the period before the advent of Christ, or in the period after the advent, or in both. Thus, dispensationally, Abraham was promised numerous descendants, "I will multiply thee exceedingly" (Gen. 17: 2). (Compare Gen. 12: 2 where at his call God said, "and I will make of thee a great nation"; and Gen. 13: 16, "I will make thy seed as the dust of the earth". See also 15: 5.) Dispensationally this promise of numerous descendants has been fulfilled in the Jewish nation and in the numerous descendants of Abraham through Ishmael and his other sons by concubines. Trans-dispensationally, that is, in the dispensation of the Spirit, in this era which we call "the last days", the promise has been fulfilled in the multitudes of believers who are the seed of Abraham, for, as Paul says in Rom. 4: 13, "The promise that he be the heir of the world was not to Abraham or his seed through the law, but through the righteousness of faith". Thus the focus of interest in the New Testament is not upon Israel according to the flesh, but upon the true seed of Abraham, those who are Christ's by faith, as Paul says in Gal. 3: 27-29. "For as many of you as have been baptised into Christ have put on Christ. There is neither Jew nor Greek, there is neither bond nor free, there is neither male nor female; for ye are all one in Christ Jesus. And if ye be Christ's *then are ye Abraham's seed*, and heirs according to the promise." So the true seed of Abraham according to Paul's teaching are believers and believers only.

Likewise, in the Old Testament dispensation, the promise of the land to Abraham and his descendants (Gen. 17: 8) was fulfilled in the gift of Canaan, but in the New Testament age of the Spirit, it is fulfilled in the believers' inheritance in Christ which, unlike the land, is "incorruptible, and undefiled and that fadeth not away, reserved in heaven for you, Who are kept by the power of God through faith unto salvation ready to be revealed in the last time" (1 Pet. 1: 4, 5). We note again the double reference to the dispensation of preparation and the dispensation of fulfilment.

Central to the Abrahamic covenant is the divine pledge: "I will establish my covenant between me and thee, and thy seed after thee in their generation, for an everlasting covenant, to be a God unto thee and thy seed after thee" (Gen. 17: 7). It is this pledge, with its principle "to thee and thy seed after thee", which is the key concept of covenant theology. The importance of it can be gauged by recalling how Calvin in his *Institutes* employed it against the Anabaptists. "They always remain caught in this dilemma. The command of God to circumcise infants was either legitimate and exempt from cavil or deserved reprehension. If there was nothing incompetent or absurd in it, no absurdity can be shown in the observance of Paedobaptism." [7]

Before we capitulate to such an onslaught of Calvinian logic we must pause and ask a question: Did not circumcision have a national reference as a mark of national separation to God; marking off Jews as a race from the nations round about?[8] If so, and this can hardly be denied, we would expect that circumcision as a rite would be performed upon not only Abraham, but upon all his male descendants as well as all who had any physical connection with his family, either the sons of his concubines or slaves purchased with his money. Genesis 17: 13, 14 makes this abundantly clear. "He that is born in thy house (*i.e. the child of a concubine*) and he that is bought with thy money (*i.e. a slave*) must needs be circumcised; and my covenant shall be in your flesh for an everlasting covenant. And the uncircumcised man child whose flesh of his foreskin is not circumcised, that soul shall be cut off from his people; he hath broken my covenant." Now it will not do to reply that circumcision had a spiritual significance and is the sign of the covenant of grace in the "highest reaches of its meaning and in its deepest spiritual significance".[9] It is this indeed, but this does not mean that its national significance as the covenant sign for all male Israelites can be quietly ignored in the interests of making circumcision identical in meaning with baptism, which of course has no national significance whatsoever. (See Gal. 3: 27-29.)

As we have pointed out already, the covenant made with Abraham contains both dispensational and trans-dispensational elements. It has both a temporal and an eternal aspect, an earthly and a heavenly substance. Circumcision, as the covenant sign in the flesh of all male Israelites, was a sign and pledge that God would be as faithful with respect to the earthly elements of the covenant promise as he would with respect to the heavenly and spiritual. Circumcision has thus a twofold reference and application. In the words of Jewett, "To him who was an Israelite indeed, who walked in the steps of Abraham's faith, his circumcision was the seal of the righteousness of his faith. Yet it belonged to all the seed of Abraham after the flesh, in so far as the covenant blessings were of an earthly sort and so it was applied to all male descendants of Abraham".[10]

Corresponding to the two aspects of the covenant with Abraham, according to the teaching of the New Testament there is a twofold seed of Abraham, as Paul makes clear in his extended discussion in Gal. 4: 21-31. He tells us that the children after the flesh (vv. 23 and 29) possessed the land, and were marked off from the nations round about them by the covenant sign of circumcision in their flesh, but they were not all born "after the Spirit" (v. 29). Indeed the children of the flesh opposed the children born after the Spirit. The principle that the children of the flesh inevitably persecute the children of the Spirit, Paul says, was operative then, and is operative now. So those who were born after the flesh, although they had an interest in the earthly blessings promised in the covenant, had no interest in the spiritual and eternal inheritance that God declared would be the lot of his own people. They belonged in a physical sense to the seed of Abraham but they were not the seed of Abraham by faith.

When it is pointed out on the basis of Gal. 4 and other passages that the Abrahamic covenant has this twofold aspect, external and internal, earthly and heavenly, Paedobaptists frequently reply with a diatribe against the extreme sinfulness of dividing the covenant. For example, Marcel says, "The device whereby an attempt is made to divide the Abrahamic covenant into two or three covenants distinct from each other in order that, to suit the convenience of certain people, a carnal element may be inserted into it, has no justification for when the Bible refers to the covenant with Abraham it always speaks of it in the singular and says covenant and not covenants".[1]

This is a gross misrepresentation; we do not divide the Abrahamic covenant into two or more covenants in the interests of demonstrating that it has a carnal element. It is certainly true that the singular noun covenant is used, but the conclusion does not follow that the Abrahamic covenant could not embrace, as it evidently did, both earthly and heavenly blessings. Why could one covenant not embrace both aspects? There is, after all, embedded within the covenant promise in Gen. 17 the promise of the land of Canaan, but not even Marcel would insist that the infant seed of believers are now promised this. (At least there is no sign that French children of the covenant are sent to Israel in order to claim their inheritance in the land!) It is also true that there is not any explicit text of Scripture which in so many words speaks of an external participation in the covenant. Nonetheless, despite Marcel's strictures there is no other interpretation that makes sense as Paedobaptists recognise when, in their better moments, they talk of external and internal participation in the covenant.[12]

Jewett is surely correct when he writes, "If the typical, external phase of the Old Testament cannot be separated from the spiritual blessings signified, then how could the spiritual blessings have survived the passing of the Old Testament types? It must be supposed, therefore, that there was a literal blessing containing within it a spiritual blessing, just as there was a literal Israel within which there was the true Israel, so that a man could be an Israelite in the former sense without being one in the latter. This is the only way to make sense of Scripture. There was a *de facto* participation in the covenant, according to which a man might be circumcised of whom no more was presupposed than that he was a member of Israel 'after the flesh'. In fact, it may be suggested that the covenant sign was administered to the organ of generation in the Old Testament for this very reason, that the covenant status was then passed on from generation to generation by physical birth. Thus the term 'seed' in the Old Testament framing of the promise had a primary reference to the fleshly seed, the notion of a spiritual seed coming into the foreground only in the New Testament." [13]

New Testament Interpretation

We must look, secondly, at the crucial matter of the New Testament interpretation of circumcision. This to me constitutes the very heart of our reply to those who would argue that the analogy of circumcision and baptism gives us a warrant to baptise children. It is clear from an examination of the New Testament interpretation of circumcision that it is its spiritual significance, not its fleshly aspect, which is in the foreground. When Paul says in Eph. 2: 11-12 that, in their pre-Christian condition his readers were in a state of uncircumcision, he was not referring to their lack of the sign in their flesh. Rather he meant that in their unregenerate state they were "without Christ, being aliens from the commonwealth of Israel and strangers from the covenant of promise". Thus, "to be in Christ must be to possess those blessings of which circumcision in the flesh was no less certainly the sign in the Old Testament, than is baptism in the New".[14] Hence the apostle can describe Gentile Christians as the circumcision who worship God in the Spirit (Phil. 3: 3), and who are Jews inwardly (Rom. 2: 29).

It is my contention that here the Paedobaptist argument is

seriously astray. These New Testament texts demonstrate that circumcision in the Old Testament is the type of which inward circumcision, *i.e.* regeneration, is the antitype. If this is so, how can it be argued that baptism is equivalent in meaning to circumcision, when circumcision in the New Testament is clearly related to regeneration? No New Testament proof can be found for the contention that baptism and circumcision are identical, and we are therefore precluded from inferring that baptism should be applied to infants. If we put circumcision in parallel with baptism are we not ignoring the fulfilment of circumcision in regeneration?

An examination of the New Testament also makes it clear that Paul's definition of spiritual circumcision allows no place whatsoever for the concept of believers *and* their infant seed. It is *believers and believers only* who are the circumcision, whereas in Israel every male according to the flesh received this sign.

I would argue then that the principle of believers and their seed no longer has covenantal significance, precisely because the age of fulfilment has arrived. The age of preparation has passed and the dispensational elements that were found in the covenant of promise in Gen. 17 are no longer operative, and it is to these dispensational elements that the principle of "thee and thy seed" is tied.

New Covenant

What indications are there in Scripture that the principle of "thee and thy seed" is abrogated in the era of the New Covenant? First there is the promise of the New Covenant (Jer. 31: 31-34). According to v. 33, God will write his law on the hearts of his people. The emphasis is shifted from the external ceremonies and institutions of the Old Covenant to the possession of inward spiritual life. (See Rom. 2: 29; Phil. 3: 3.) It is those who know the life of God within their souls to whom the promise, "they shall be my people", applies.

The next verse indicates another point of distinction between the Old and New Covenants. Many who received the sign of circumcision were without the knowledge of God (Rom. 2: 17-29), whereas under the New Covenant God declares "they shall all know me, from the least of them unto the greatest of them". In the New Testament this universal knowledge of God through vital communion with him in the Holy Spirit is predicated of the *visible* church of believers (cf. 2 Cor. 6: 16).

34

Nowhere in the content of the New Covenant is the principle "thee and thy seed" mentioned.[15] On the contrary there is a stress upon the inwardness of spiritual experience and a common knowledge of God that makes the absence of any mention of the seed perfectly understandable. To have preserved the principle of automatic covenant membership by birth would have wrought untold confusion between the physical requirements for membership in the nation of Israel and the spiritual demands of the New Covenant. Isaiah points out that the eunuch who was disqualified from membership in the congregation of Israel (Deut. 23: 1) is, in the Messianic age, to have within God's house "an everlasting name, that shall not be cut off" (56: 4, 5). As E. J. Young observes, "Inasmuch as the Lord's salvation is near, all personal and national distinctions and disabilities are to be abolished".[16]

Baptism of John

Secondly, the principle of birth connection is clearly abrogated in the baptism of John. His was a baptism of repentance (Mark 1: 4). He admitted to baptism only those who confessed their sins (Matt. 3: 6). Those capable of confessing their sins are clearly not infants, as Paedobaptist writers such as Francis Turretine appreciate, "John admitted none to baptism but those who confessed their sins; because his business was to baptise adults".[17] John 3: 22, 26 and 4: 1 indicate that the disciples of Jesus, no doubt acting on his instructions, followed the same practice. If John baptised only those who could confess their sins, and if the disciples of our Lord followed the same practice, why should it be so difficult to believe that the apostolic Church did *not* practise infant baptism?

According to the Paedobaptist argument, John should have baptised infants as well as adults since he would, as a Jew, have accepted the principle of "thee and thy seed". Yet he did not baptise infants. How do Paedobaptists account for this? I suggest that on their own premises they are caught in a very difficult position. They could maintain, firstly, that since John did not baptise infants without a clear command *not* to do so, he had acted without divine authorisation. This is unthinkable in the light of his mission as God's messenger (Mark 1: 2).

Secondly, Paedobaptists could argue that in the case of his repentance-baptism the principle did not apply. If they choose to argue in this way they must show why the principle should not apply to Christian baptism which is also, among other things, a repentance-baptism (*e.g.* Acts 2: 38).

It seems to me that there can be no escape for Paedobaptists from the dilemma posed by John's baptism. Either John baptised infants (which they admit he did not) or he did not uphold the covenant principle of "thee and thy seed". If he did not uphold this principle, then it was by no means obvious to John that it continued in force until it was explicitly brought to an end by God. If John did not uphold it, then why should it be insisted that our Lord and his apostles did?

John's baptism makes sense only within the development of redemptive revelation when it is realised that his ministry marked the transition from the old to the new dispensations. Thus Mark views his ministry as "the beginning of the Gospel of Jesus Christ, the Son of God" (Mark 1: 1). If at the beginning of the gospel of Christ the principle of birth connection was abandoned, why should it be resurrected to justify infant baptism?

When the blessings of the Gospel were extended to the Gentiles the principle of "thee and thy seed after thee" was further seen to have been abrogated in the literal sense, for "seed" in the case of the Gentiles cannot be made to mean that the Gentile inheritors of the promise are literally (*i.e.* in a physical sense) descended from Abraham. If then they descend from Abraham in a *spiritual sense only*, in that they walk in the steps of his faith (Rom. 4: 12, 16), why should their children be held to inherit the promise *through their physical bond* with their parents? Surely the abrogation of the principle in the literal sense in the case of the Gentiles means that it is abrogated for their children as well.

NOTES

1. *Christian Baptism*, pp. 51-2. "Inhabile" is used in the sense of unfit or unqualified.
2. Pierre Charles Marcel, *The Biblical Doctrine of Infant Baptism*, James Clarke, London, 1953, p. 191. English translation by Philip Edgcumbe Hughes of *Le Baptemé* (1950).
3. Karl Barth, *The Teaching of the Church Regarding Baptism*, English translation by E. A. Payne, S.C.M., London, 1948.

4. James Bannerman, *The Church of Christ,* Banner of Truth Trust reprint (1950) of 1869 edition, II, p. 85, "as the signs and seals of the same covenant blessings, circumcision and Baptism are one and the same".

5. See G. R. Beasley-Murray, *Baptism in the New Testament,* MacMillan, London, revised edition, 1963, p. 152 ff. J. O. Buswell, Jr., contends strongly for the meaning "Christian circumcision", *i.e.* he takes "te peritomē tou Christou" as an attributive genitive, *A Systematic Theology of the Christian Religion,* Zondervan, Grand Rapids, 1963, Vol. 2.

6. Jewett, *Baptism and Confirmation,* pp. 168-9.

7. *Institutes of the Christian Religion,* Beveridge's translation, James Clarke, London, 1953, Bk. IV, chap. 16, para. 20.

8. Paedobaptists readily admit this when it suits their purposes to do so, and then just as readily forget it when it does not. See Hodge, *Systematic Theology,* Vol. 3, pp. 553-5 in contrast to James Bannerman, *The Church of Christ,* Vol. 2, pp. 80-6.

9. John Murray, op. cit., p. 49.

10. Jewett, op. cit., p. 184.

11. Marcel, op. cit., p. 87.

12. "It is clearer than the day," says Thomas Shepard, "that many who are inwardly, or in respect of inward covenant, the children of the devil, are outwardly, or in respect of outward covenant, the children of God." *The Church Membership of Children,* reprinted in *The Reformation of the Church,* edited by Iain Murray, Banner of Truth Trust, London, 1965, p. 383. Shepard's whole argument in favour of infant baptism turns upon this distinction.

13. Jewett, op. cit., pp. 185-6.

14. Jewett, op. cit., p. 167.

15. This is the more striking in that the Sinaitic covenant *explicitly* took up this principle (cf. Lev. 12: 3; Exod. 12: 48). If it still held good one would have expected (by analogy) that it would have been explicitly incorporated within the New Covenant.

16. E. J. Young, *The Book of Isaiah,* Eerdmans, Grand Rapids, 1972, Vol. 3, pp. 390-1.

17. *Institutes of Theology,* Section IV, question 22, quoted T. E. Watson, *Baptism Not For Infants,* 1962, reprinted Henry Walter, 1972, p. 22.

CHAPTER 3

A CRITIQUE OF COVENANT THEOLOGY

In the two previous chapters we have seen what is the main thrust of covenant theology. In particular we have noticed the inferential character of the argument for infant baptism, namely, that since children were included within the covenant God made with Abraham, and since that covenant has not been annulled, but rather expanded in the New Testament, it is unthinkable that infants should now be excluded from it. Since infants are still included within the covenant, they ought, as the seed of believers, to be granted baptism. It is now my task to offer a criticism of the argument, but I do so because of a hearty commitment to Reformed theology, desiring to emphasise to both Reformed Paedobaptists and non-Reformed Baptists that it is possible to be Reformed and Baptist.

Wrong Method

My criticisms may be set out as follows. Firstly, I would argue that the covenantal theologians employ the wrong method. This is my starting point, since the proponents of covenant theology have a definite method of approach which governs their exegesis of Scripture. Fundamental to their approach is a rightful conviction of the unity of the covenant of grace throughout both dispensations. Without question Scripture does exhibit this unity. The substance of the covenant is declared in both Testaments to be the blessing God graciously bestowed upon his people, as contained in the promise "I will be your God". However, it is my conviction that the unity of the covenant has been wrenched to the point of distortion. In particular, the relationship between promise and fulfilment is wrongly interpreted. Instead of the fulfilment of the covenant promises in Christ being viewed as far richer than the Old Testament types and shadows there is an inveterate tendency in Paedobaptist theology to speak and write in terms of their identity. This is particularly the case, as we have seen, with circumcision. Paedobaptists stress, when it suits their purpose to do so, that the rite had a natural and national significance as well as a profound spiritual meaning. But though the natural and national significance which is part of the temporal and earthly aspect of the covenant blessing has now passed away, it keeps reappearing unacknowledged in Paedobaptist apologetic. Thus the concept of a literal seed of believers is carried over into the New Testament without recognition of the fact that the New Testament interpretation of the seed of Abraham does not permit the notion of "believers *and* their children" to be included in it. When Paul defines the seed of Abraham he defines it in terms of believers and believers *only*. The seed of Abraham are those who have embraced Christ by faith, and only those (Gal. 3: 7).

I have been replied to on this point by the Rev. J. L. Heaney in the *Gospel Magazine* for April, 1968, but Mr. Heaney's reply illustrates the point that I am making. He writes, "I cannot see that because believers only (he admits this) are to be reckoned as the seed of Abraham, there should be any difficulty of their having the privilege accorded to Abraham in the matter of including their seed within the covenant relationship. If, as Gal. 3: 26, 29 avers, believers are heirs according to the promise, why should they be denied that part of the promise which relates to 'thy seed after thee'" (Gen. 17: 7)?[1] If Mr. Heaney's argument is correct it invites the question, "How far he is prepared to apply it?" We may ask why, on Mr. Heaney's own reasoning, believers should be excluded from that part of the promise which relates "to all the land of Canaan for an everlasting possession", particularly since this element of the promise occurs both within the context of the declaration, "I will give (it) to you, and to your seed after you", *and* "I will be their God".

Here we can see a typical example of the method of covenantal theologians of the Paedobaptist type, an example which illustrates the point that they are dwelling in the sphere of the theocracy of Israel rather than in the realm of the redeemed community, the Church. Mr. Heaney is prepared to drop the "land" out of the promise of God to Abraham, but he is not prepared to drop the infant seed of Abraham and say, as he would in the case of the land, that we must understand it in the way the New Testament does as the believer's inheritance in Christ (1 Pet. 1 : 4). Now if he does this in the one case, why is he not prepared to do it in the other, particularly when the New Testament offers us the clearest possible definition of what is meant by the seed of Abraham? In short then, we are maintaining that the Reformed Paedobaptist is incorrect in his method of approach to the covenant. Whilst rightly stressing its unity, he often overlooks the diversity of its administration, which arises because we have passed from the age of types and shadows into the last days.

Jewett aptly describes the point that I have been trying to make, "In the Old Testament dispensation though the promise of salvation then, as now, had its foundation in Christ, yet to encourage the Old Testament saints to hope in the celestial inheritance, God condescended to their weakness by exhibiting the promise of eternal life for their partial contemplation and enjoyment under the figure of temporal and terrestrial blessing. This temporal and terrestrial aspect of the covenant blessing has now passed away; it has dropped from the great house of salvation like scaffolding from a finished edifice".[2] Basically, then, covenant theology fails at this point in the area of hermeneutics. Its proponents are guilty, I believe, of using a wrong hermeneutical method which results in a failure properly to understand the relationship between the Old and New Testaments.

Another failure in method lies in the use that is made of the inference from circumcision to baptism. Paedobaptists, whilst they claim no express warrant for the practice of infant baptism in the New Testament, have frequently argued that the inference is of such a compelling nature that only an express command *not* to baptise infants would establish and be sufficient to prove the Baptist position. Frank Colquhoun, for example, writes, "The Old Testament argument is the main argument, the conclusive argument, the only real justification for this doctrine. The New Testament facts, let me repeat, are not the primary proof. They are the most important corroborative proofs and from that point of view they are indispensable. They certainly establish and confirm the Scriptural authority for practising infant baptism, but they do not prove it; indeed it may be said quite frankly that so long as we keep to the New Testament alone and ignore the Old Testament it is impossible to prove this doctrine".[3] It is interesting to see that Colquhoun precedes his chapter on the covenant principle with one on the New

40

Testament evidence for infant baptism. This suggests that he is in fact not happy to rest his entire case on the Old Testament. In other words, the Paedobaptist's search for hints from the New Testament to justify his practice is evidence that he is not really persuaded that the inference from circumcision is as compelling as he claims. If it were so, no New Testament corroboration would, in principle, be necessary since its complete silence would be the clearest evidence that the covenantal principle of "thee and thy seed" was so taken for granted that the New Testament writers had no cause whatsoever to notice infant baptism as being of any special significance. As I pointed out in the previous chapter, Marcel argues in this fashion—"the silence of the New Testament militates in favour of rather than against this practice".[4] Strangely enough, Paedobaptists never tire of trying to break the silence of the New Testament to back up their argument from circumcision. They surely would not do so if they were as convinced of it as they proclaim themselves to be.[5]

Moreover, many Reformed Paedobaptists appeal to the practice of proselyte baptism in Judaism to support their basic argument without realising that, in fact, it contradicts it. While it is true that when proselytes were received into Judaism, not only adults but also their children were immersed, this, far from proving the case for the practice of infant baptism based upon covenant theology, actually demolishes it. For the fact is that children born *after* the reception of their parents into the fold of Judaism were not baptised, on the ground that they were in the father's loins at the time of his baptism.[6] The Paedobaptist's case would be proved only if children born subsequent to their parents' conversion were baptised. Proselyte baptism is a conversion rite which supplies no analogy for the practice of baptising infants who are held to stand within the covenant by virtue of their birth as the children of believers. The very fact that Douglas Bannerman[7] and others should appeal to the practice of proselyte baptism in the way they do, shows again that there is an inner doubt in their minds about the compelling nature of the inference from circumcision as the foundation for infant baptism.

Reading New Testament Into Old

The second point I would make is that Reformed Paedobaptist theologians are guilty of reading the New Testament into the Old.

Paedobaptist apologetic is very difficult to control, and for this reason, it switches from the New to the Old and from the Old back to the New without proper attention to the historical unfolding of redemptive grace. Jewett pinpoints the issue for us, "It is our contention that the Paedobaptists, in framing their great argument from circumcision have failed to keep the significant historical development in clear focus. Proceeding from the basically correct postulate that baptism stands in the place of circumcision, they have argued this analogy to a distortion. They have so far pressed the unity of the covenant as to suppress the diversity of its administration. They have, to be specific, Christianised the Old Testament and Judaised the New. It is this double movement within the argument from circumcision—reading the New Testament as though it were the Old and the Old as though it were the New—which makes it so easy to use and so difficult to control".[8] As I have pointed out before, Paedobaptists rightly state that circumcision was not exclusively a national sign, but they do not really stop to define in what sense it was a national and in what sense it was a spiritual sign.

The crux of the matter is whether or not participation in the temporal, earthly blessings of the covenant was sufficient in the Old Testament period to give a right to circumcision. One notices a marked tendency not to give an unequivocal "yes" to that enquiry, for an obvious reason. If Paedobaptists say categorically that participation in the earthly, temporal blessings of the covenant was sufficient, then they destroy the identity which they have maintained exists between circumcision and baptism, for they insist that baptism should be applied only to *believers* and their seed, not to all and sundry. The New Testament evidence for believers' baptism is, at this point, too compelling to be ignored. If, on the other hand they say "No", then they have to maintain that the man not only had to be a Jew by natural descent from Abraham, but that he also had to walk personally in the steps of Abraham's faith, in order that he might be circumcised with his children.

Herbert S. Bird has attempted to meet this difficulty by pointing out that in the Old Testament there are provisions for the disciplining of Israelites which challenge, as he thinks, the assumption that "quite irrespective of any consideration of his attitude towards the claims of the God of Israel upon his life, a Jew, as a Jew was entitled to the national badge and participation in the organised life of the covenant community".[9] An Israelite, he points out, could be "cut off from among his people" (that is, executed) for the following offences: eating of unleavened bread during the Passover season (Exod. 12: 15); murder (Exod. 21: 12); idolatry (Exod. 22: 20); misuse of the holy anointing oil (Exod. 30: 33); sabbath breaking (Exod. 31: 14); transgression of the laws of sacrifice (Lev. 17 passim); sexual crimes (Lev. 18: 29); blasphemy (Lev. 24: 15, 16) and numerous others.

However, with respect, we must point out that Mr. Bird has not really met the difficulty. Granted that participation in the earthly temporal blessings of the covenant could be brought to an end by the exercise of discipline for the offences mentioned, it still remains that the basis upon which any male Israelite participated in these blessings was simply circumcision in his flesh as a member of the nation of Israel. I submit that Mr. Bird cannot prove what his argument tacitly assumes, namely, that a confession of personal faith was necessary to ensure the enjoyment of the temporal blessings of the covenant. In some countries, a murderer proved guilty is executed. Would his execution, his being cut off from the nation, be proof that at some time or another he had had to make a confession of faith in order to obtain the benefits of his nationality? Not at all! Those benefits were obtained by virtue of his birth into his nation. Likewise, the citizen of Israel was born into the enjoyment of national privileges without being required personally to confess his faith. What Mr. Bird does is to read the New Testament requirement of faith for baptism and membership of the Church into the Old Testament theocracy when he writes, "The *unbeliever*, the impenitent sinner or the patent hypocrite was to be dealt with in such a way that after his delinquency had become known and was proved, the question of whether or not his male issue was entitled to the covenant sign became purely academic"[10] (my italics). I am afraid that there is an air of unreality about this statement. The delinquent was cut off as a breaker of the law of the theocracy, not as an unbeliever in the New Testament sense. Furthermore, if any man suffered damage to his sexual organs through no fault of his own, however much he might have believed with faithful Abraham, he was not allowed to be a member of the congregation of Israel (Deut. 23: 1), a fact which strongly suggests that physical reasons were sufficient to ensure participation in the covenant people of Israel.

43

We find another instance of the tendency to read the New Testament into the Old in the way in which the account of the institution of circumcision is handled in Genesis 17. Where is there any hint in verses 10 to 14, that any of the males in Abraham's household, be they his retainers or his slaves, or the sons of his concubines, were required to make a personal confession of faith in Abraham's God before being circumcised? Where is there any suggestion that a man born of Abraham's seed might disqualify his children from circumcision if he did not exercise the faith of Abraham? If, on the other hand, it is conceded that not all the males of Abraham's household were asked for a confession of faith in Abraham's God, did Abraham, who was the only person of whose circumcision it is explicitly said that it was the sign and seal of his faith (Rom. 4: 11), exercise faith on their behalf as the head of the group and the one with whom the covenant was made? If so, and this would be the most natural interpretation of Genesis 17, it would prove far too much for the Paedobaptists, since it would mean that even now servants could be baptised by virtue of the fact that the head of the household is a believer.

There was a great deal of discussion in the days of slave-owning in the U.S.A. as to whether the negro slaves of a Christian slave-owner should be baptised. The very fact that there was such discussion suggests that some persons at least realised the direction in which Gen. 17: 10-14 points. If the Paedobaptists reply that the principle that the head of the household may exercise faith for *all* the members of his household, including servants, is no longer in operation, we must ask him where in the New Testament it is abrogated and set aside. Can it be possible, we may ask, employing their own argument against them, that God is less generous to servants in the present dispensation than in the Old?

Meredith Kline, in his book *By Oath Consigned*, unwittingly gives away the position. He points out that, "The Covenant of Redemption in its organisation and operation avails itself of the structures and processes in which man's cultural history unfolds. It does so, however, in different ways in different ages".[11]

"In Old Testament times the redemptive covenant actually embodied itself in one or other cultural *authority* structure. These cultural units did not comprise the unbroken totality of culture as in the pre-redemptive age, but the covenant and the particular cultural unit did coalesce. As *authority* structures they were one and co-

44

extensive. Thus, the structure of the Abrahamic covenant was identical with that of the patriarch's authority sphere. And since the covenant took over as its own structure the existing social structure with Abraham as the head of the *household* community, Abraham was also head over the covenantal community, and covenantal government included (even at the human level) cultural and physical sanctions"[12] (my italics).

Kline is quite correct here. He is saying that Abraham, as the head of the household, involved every male member (and indeed every female member also) in his allegiance to God, and in virtue of this the males were circumcised, not because Abraham's faith was required of them, but because they happened to be within the authority structure of which he was the head. If this is so, and I think Kline has proved his point admirably, why do the Paedobaptists talk of the adult members of Abraham's household as though they were all New Testament believers? Why do they point to the spiritual significance of circumcision as if this modified in any way the authority structure over which Abraham was head? The answer is quite clear, they read into the Genesis narrative the New Testament requirement of faith for baptism, as they must do if they are to establish an analogy between baptism and circumcision in terms of complete identity. They try to Christianise the institution of circumcision, but their argument is basically unsound.

Further evidences of the awkwardness of the Old Testament data as it is made to fit into the Paedobaptist scheme, are the circumcisions of Ishmael, the sons of Keturah, and Esau. Ishmael we learn was given the sign of the covenant (Gen. 17: 25) yet he was expressly excluded from the blessings of the covenant (Rom. 9: 7; Gal. 4: 24-31). The child of the bondwoman was cast out, yet he received the covenant sign. Why? In attempting to answer this question Paedobaptists face a difficulty. If circumcision has precisely the same meaning as baptism, then what is its meaning in the case of Ishmael? "What in baptism," asks Jewett, "corresponds to Ishmael's circumcision? It is as easy to go from Christian baptism back to Isaac's circumcision as it is difficult to go from Christian baptism back to Ishmael's circumcision. All this points out how the alignment between circumcision and baptism in the Paedobaptist scheme is overdrawn."[13] Professor John Murray's reply to this point is to say that Ishmael was circumcised because to leave him uncircumcised would have been to violate the command to circumcise all male members of the household.[14] This is no doubt true, but it still fails to explain why the covenant sign should have been given to Ishmael who was not a believer and was not therefore, by definition, in the covenant. In Paedobaptist apologetic we hear of those who voluntarily put themselves out of the covenant by their unbelief, but never of covenant children who have received the covenant sign, but were never offered the blessings of the covenant.

Reading Old Testament Into New

We have noticed already that the stream of Paedobaptist apologetic exhibits the remarkable property of flowing in opposite directions at once. We have argued already that external national privilege was, in the Old Testament, a sufficient ground for circumcision. We would now urge that we should not intrude such external privilege into the New Testament as a sufficient ground for baptism, since to do so would be to Judaise the New Covenant. We may get this matter into focus by quoting from the *Directory for the Public Worship of God*, which the Westminster divines produced. "The seed and posterity of the faithful born within the Church, have by their *birth* interest in the covenant and right to the seal of it, and to the outward privileges of the church under the Gospel, no less than the children of Abraham in the time of the Old Testament"[15] (italics mine). Thus children of the covenant are determined purely by birth in the same literal fashion that all the members of the Jewish nation were children of the covenant because they were born of Abraham according to the flesh. Jewett comments acidly, "All the child needs, to be counted among God's people is to be born of blood, the will of the flesh and of man, provided the man gives evidence of himself being a believer".[16]

Calvin demonstrates how easily Paedobaptists leap over the centuries of covenantal revelation from Abraham to the New Testament. He rightly points out that Abraham received the sign of circumcision only after he had embraced the promise by faith, whereas Isaac received the sign of the covenant prior to the exercise of understanding and faith. This is because the child, "according to the terms of the promise, is included in the promise from his mother's womb". Quite so, but then he proceeds to draw this inference: "If the children of believers, without the help of understanding, are partakers of the covenant, there is no reason why they should be denied the sign because they are unable to swear to its stipulations".[17] But have our children, we must ask, a hereditary right to salvation? Is grace tied to the blood? Surely not, on the basis of John 1:12. Significantly many Paedobaptists have betrayed the theocratic cast of their minds by the way in which they argue at this very point.

Charles Hodge, for example, writes, "If the father becomes a citizen of a country he makes his children citizens. In like manner when a man becomes a Christian his children are to be regarded as doing the same thing. When any foreigner became a Jew, his children became Jews (Exod. 12:48). The church membership of infants of believers is therefore in accordance with the analogy of all human social institutions and sanctioned by the approbation and command of God. By becoming an English citizen a man makes his infant children subjects of the English crown, entitled to the protection and privileges, and burdened with the obligations of English citizenship".[18] One can compare with this the following statement of Professor Murray, "Baptised infants are to be received as the children of God and treated accordingly".[19] On this argument a man is a Christian merely because his parents are Christians, just as in the Old Testament those born into Israel were naturally Jews! Yet surely it is crystal clear that, while a man was a Jew (in the age of type and shadow) by birth, he is not a Jew inwardly (in the age of fulfilment) in any other way than by the new birth (Rom. 9:7; cf. 2:28, 29). According to the New Testament, only those who share Abraham's faith are Abraham's seed (Gal. 3:29). Inclusion within this seed cannot be secured by the faith of parents, nor can the unbelief of parents deprive their children of membership, if they are among the elect of God.

When Paedobaptists are not defending infant baptism they are prepared to admit this. Calvin, for instance, recognises that there are "certain distinct degrees of adoption". "Here, then, a twofold class of sons presents itself to us, in the (Old Testament) Church; for since the whole body of the people is gathered into the fold of God, by one and the same voice, all without exception, are, *in this respect*, accounted children; the name of the (Old Testament) Church is applicable in common to them all: but in the innermost sanctuary of God, none others are reckoned the sons of God, than they in whom the promise is ratified by faith"[20] (my italics).

NOTES

1. *Gospel Magazine*, New Series, No. 1387.
2. Jewett, *Encyclopaedia of Christianity*, Vol. 7, p. 524.
3. F. Colquhoun, *Is Infant Baptism Scriptural?* Falcon Booklets, revised edition, 1962, p. 9.

   It is interesting to note that Paedobaptists employ the argument from silence in exactly the opposite way when in controversy with the Church of Rome. For example, Boettner writes: "Since the priesthood occupied such an important place in the Old Testament dispensation and in the thinking of the Jewish people, *it is inconceivable that had it been continued in the New Testament dispensation God would have made no mention of it* at all . . ." (L. Boettner: *Roman Catholicism*, Presbyterian and Reformed, Philadelphia, 1962, p. 48) (my italics). Thus against Rome Paedobaptists insist: There is no positive command to continue the Old Testament priesthood, therefore it is *not* in force, whereas against the Baptists they declare that though there is no positive command to baptise infants, the Old Testament command to circumcise infants still holds good, and provides a warrant for infant baptism. So the argument from silence is used in two contradictory ways:

   (1) Against Rome: No positive command, therefore the institution no longer continues;

   (2) Against Baptists: No positive command, therefore the institution continues.
4. Marcel, *op. cit.*, p. 191.
5. The argument from silence to establish the case for infant baptism may be challenged on other counts. Firstly, Gen. 17: 1-14 sanctions only the circumcision of male children. Since in the New Testament there is no express command to baptise females, and since the Jewish people of the day would have followed the prevailing practice, only male adults and male children should have been baptised. The fact that there are examples of the baptism of women in the New Testament (*e.g.* Lydia, Acts 16: 15) only serves to underline the problems surrounding the argument from silence. If a change so momentous took place why do we not find an express warrant authorising it? If Paedobaptists insist so strenuously against the Baptists upon an express warrant prohibiting the baptism of infants they can scarcely complain if Baptists demand an express warrant authorising the baptism of females.

   Secondly, since children partook of the Passover meal in Old Testament times, why are baptised children now denied participation in the Lord's Supper, which is analogous to it? Where in the New Testament is there express warrant sanctioning their exclusion? Is not the silence of the New Testament an incontrovertible argument in favour of infant communion?
6. See H. H. Rowley, *The Unity of the Bible*, Carey Kingsgate Press, London, 1953, pp. 154-5.
7. Douglas Bannerman, *Difficulties About Baptism*, (1898), Reprinted by the Presbyterian Fellowship, Belfast.
8. Jewett, *Baptism*, p. 171.
9. "Professor Jewett on Baptism," *Westminster Theological Journal*, Vol. 31, pp. 158-9.
10. *ibid.*, p. 159.
11. Meredith G. Kline, *By Oath Consigned*, Eerdmans, Grand Rapids, U.S.A., 1968, pp. 97-8, leaves open the possibility that servants should be bap-

tised, but he adds, "Perhaps the complications that can easily be foreseen developing in this area are in themselves sufficient to turn us from further consideration of this approach as a proper interpretation of New Testament directives, or in any case to lead us to judge the procedure as generally inexpedient, should we be of the opinion that the New Testament at least permitted it" (p. 98). The embarrassment of Professor Kline is all too obvious.

12. *ibid.,* pp. 99-100.
13. Jewett, *op. cit.,* p. 180.
14. Murray, *op. cit.,* p. 60.
15. *Of the Administration of the Sacraments.*
16. Jewett, *op. cit.,* p. 201.
17. *Institutes,* Bk. IV, chap. 16, para. 24.
18. "The Church Membership of Infants," *Princeton Review,* Vol. 30, quoted Jewett.
19. *Christian Baptism,* p. 59.
20. *A Commentary on Genesis,* English translation by John King, Banner of Truth Trust edition, 1965, at Genesis 17: 7.

CHAPTER 4

TOWARDS A BAPTIST THEOLOGY OF THE COVENANT

It would be helpful to begin this chapter by recalling some of the steps in my argument thus far.

Firstly, I have argued that covenantal Paedobaptists should not be allowed to have the monopoly of covenant theology, since many Baptists both past and present have practised, and still practise, believers' baptism within the context of covenant theology.

Secondly, I have urged the need to provide an interpretation of believers' baptism which does justice to the truly biblical insights of covenant theology.

Before embarking on the task of working out a Baptist theology of the covenant I must reiterate the principle that the New Testament must be permitted to interpret the Old, that the light of Christ's fulfilment must be seen to shine upon the shadows and types of the old dispensation. Thus I have maintained, over against the Paedobaptists' contention, that the literal seed of Abraham are still covenantally significant, that the New Testament must be allowed to define for us the meaning of the "seed of Abraham" in the dispensation in which the church now lives.

The New Testament Interpretation of the Covenant

In setting out a Baptist theology of the covenant I want to consider, first of all, the New Testament interpretation of the covenant. The covenant of God with Abraham does not fall out of sight in the New Testament. Rather, it is in the foreground of New Testament theology, especially in the Pauline epistles. The promise to Abraham, Paul tells us, has now come upon those Gentiles, who, like Jews who are believers in Christ, walk in the steps of the faith of Abraham. The promise which Abraham believed while yet being uncircumcised (Rom. 4: 10), of which circumcision is the sign and seal, now embraces Gentiles who have not been circumcised.

"It is sure to all his seed" (Rom. 4: 16). Likewise the blessing of justification before God and apart from works is now enjoyed by all those who are, as Paul says, "of faith" (Gal. 3: 9). The blessing of Abraham, that is, the blessing promised to him (Gen. 12: 2, 3) is through Christ (Rom. 4: 14), the promise of the Spirit through faith. This promise is given to, and its reality entered into by all those who believe (Rom. 4: 22).

If the promise to Abraham was made to him and to his seed it is to be expected that the New Testament will interpret the meaning of that "seed" in the present dispensation. This we find is exactly what is given us in the New Testament. We discover that it interprets the seed of Abraham in a very precise and specific manner, so that we are left in no doubt whatsoever as to its meaning. If the New Testament provides us with this interpretation then we must be guided by it as we read Old Testament passages such as Gen. 17. We cannot read them now as if the New Testament had never been written.

Since the New Testament interpretation of the seed of Abraham expressly includes, as we shall see, believers and believers *only,* and not believers *and* their children in virtue of the children's birth to Christian parents, we have the reason why there is no express command in the New Testament prohibiting the baptism of infants. None was needed, since the New Testament believers were taught that the seed of Abraham were no longer included within the covenant as once they had been, but that the spiritual seed of Abraham are believers in Christ. Why should an express command prohibiting the baptism of infants on the ground of their birth to Christian parents be necessary when the seed of Abraham is clearly defined in the New Testament as being restricted to believers only? The only way to escape this conclusion, it seems to me, is to attempt to modify the New Testament definition of the seed of Abraham so that it can be made, somehow, to include believers' children. I would suggest that the argument from silence, of which our Paedo-baptist brethren make so much, turns out to be not an eloquent but an empty silence.[1] If there is no express command prohibiting the baptism of infants, neither is there a clear statement in the New Testament that Christian believers are no longer to expect a literal inheritance in the land of Canaan. Once, however, it is realised that the promise of the land (Gen. 17: 8) is fulfilled in the spiritual inheritance that believers enjoy in Christ (1 Pet. 1: 4), no such statement is seen to be needed. If Paedobaptists are prepared to accept, as they are, the validity of this type of interpretation, why should they not be prepared to do so in the case of the seed of Abraham, for it is interpreted in exactly the same way in the New Testament—that is, as fulfilled in the spiritual or true seed of Abraham? [2]

In order to appreciate to the full the way in which the New Testament writers interpret the concept of the seed of Abraham, we need to examine their writings in more detail than we have done so far. The term "seed" or "descendants of Abraham" is used in three senses in the New Testament. Firstly, it is used of the Seed who is Christ. Paul argues in Gal. 3: 16 ff. that Christ is the seed of Abraham. The rabbinical writers, with a true spiritual insight, saw that "the Christ" who was promised was the true seed of Abraham. "In him," writes Lightfoot, "the race was summed up, as it were. In him it fulfilled its purpose and became a blessing to the whole earth. Without him its separate existence as a peculiar people had no meaning. Thus he was not only the representative but the embodiment of the race. In this way the people of Israel is the type of Christ, and in the New Testament parallels are sought in respect of the one to the life of the other."[3] Secondly, there is the literal seed of Abraham. Paul, when speaking of the natural children of Abraham, i.e. of his physical descendants, uniformly uses the Greek word *sperma* (seed) not *tekna* (children) which he always reserves for believers in Christ. If the Greek Testament be consulted at Rom. 9: 7, the distinction can be clearly seen: "Neither because they are *sperma* of Abraham, are they all *tekna*: but, In Isaac shall thy seed be called". The same basic distinction is to be found in John 8: 37 and 39. Our Lord said to the Jews, "I know that ye are Abraham's *sperma*; but ye seek to kill me, because my word hath no place in you". "They answered and said unto him, Abraham is our father. Jesus said unto them, If ye were Abraham's *tekna*, ye would do the works of Abraham." We may also note Matt. 3: 9, "And think not to say within yourselves, We have Abraham to our father: for I say unto you, that God is able of these stones to raise up *tekna* unto Abraham." The same differentiation between a literal seed and a spiritual seed is to be found in Gal. 4: 21-31. Thirdly, there is the true seed or spiritual seed of Abraham. Paul quotes the expression "so shall thy seed be" (Gen. 15: 18) to show that Abraham is the father of many nations, that is, of a great host of believers drawn out of every race and tribe and kindred who walk in the steps of his faith (Rom. 4: 18). It is to this seed, this true seed, that the promise in Rom. 4: 16 is made sure. "Therefore it is of faith, that it might be by grace; to the end the promise might be sure (or established) to all the seed; not to that only which is the law, but to that also which is of the faith of Abraham; who is the father of us all." In case we are in any doubt, in Rom. 9: 7 Paul says that only some of the literal seed are also to be found among the spiritual seed, only the children of the promise, "Neither, because they are the seed of Abraham, are they all children: but, In Isaac shall thy seed be called". In Gal. 3: 29 Paul is yet more specific, stating that those who are Christ's, *i.e.* those who are in faith-union with him (v. 28) are Abraham's seed.

In the New Testament then, it is Christ as the seed of Abraham and believers as the spiritual seed of Abraham who are in the foreground. The New Testament nowhere allows us to operate with the concept of a literal seed in the context of the church, but this is just what Paedobaptists constantly try to do. They say that our children *in the flesh* are reckoned by God to be his children too, yet this is precisely what God did not do in the case of Abraham's children. As there was an Israel after the flesh (1 Cor. 10: 18) in the Old Testament, so also, according to Paedobaptists, there are now Christians after the flesh. One would have thought, to listen to their pleas, that John 1: 12, 13 "to them gave he power to become the sons of God, even to them that believe on his name: which were born, not of blood, nor of the will of the flesh, nor of the will of man, but of God", had never been written.

Next, we must examine the New Testament understanding of circumcision. Here, again, we find that the covenant sign of circumcision is approached along the same lines as the concept of the seed of Abraham. In other words, corresponding to the threefold sense of the seed of Abraham there is a threefold sense of circumcision. Firstly, as some recent writers have argued, the phrase "the circumcision of Christ" (Col. 2: 11) may be understood as a gruesome metaphor for his atoning death. Their view is that Paul is drawing a contrast between the stripping of flesh from a single member of the body and the stripping off of the body of Christ by death. However, it is difficult to feel convinced by the arguments advanced to sustain this interpretation. In the first place it must be remembered that Paul, in the passage under consideration, is countering Jewish teachers who were advocating the necessity of circumcision. Elsewhere he insists that Christians have received a circumcision that is not external but inward and spiritual (cf. Rom. 3: 29; Phil. 3: 3). It is hard to see why he should have departed from this view when countering the same erroneous teaching. Furthermore, he makes an implied contrast between the circumcision made with hands (which is purely external) and the inward circumcision of regeneration, which involves "the putting off of the body of the flesh".

Moreover, as Ralph Martin points out, "This view is hard to accept, chiefly because it provides no reason for Paul's recourse to the strange phrases he uses. Would the Colossian readers make the intended connexion of thought, 'circumcision of Christ'=his death; 'you were circumcised'=you shared in the benefits of that sacrifice, unless there was some reason hidden in the background of the Colossian situation?"[4]

It seems better, then, to accept the more usual interpretation that Col. 2: 11 is referring to inward circumcision which consists in the spiritual and moral regeneration of a man. It is to this circumcision of the heart that Old Testament circumcision points. It is in this that it finds its fulfilment in Christ.

In the second place there is, by contrast, circumcision made by hands (Eph. 2: 11), without an accompanying inward circumcision of the heart, merely external in the flesh.

Thirdly, there is spiritual circumcision. This circumcision, as opposed to literal circumcision, is inward, as Paul says, "of the heart, in the spirit and not in the letter" (Rom. 2: 29). Thus, of the church of Christ, Paul can say with glad confidence, "We are the circumcision which worship God in the spirit and rejoice in Christ Jesus, and have no confidence in the flesh" (Phil. 3: 3).

If believers are the spiritual seed of Abraham, then it follows that they are spiritually circumcised. One could not belong to the spiritual seed, the true seed of Abraham, without receiving spiritual circumcision, the two go together. This might appear to mean that no outward covenant sign is now needed, but this is not the case. Baptism has been instituted as the mark for all who are the seed of Abraham. In its spiritual and ethical significance Christian baptism takes over and deepens the spiritual and ethical significance of Old Testament circumcision, but it does not take over its national and fleshly meaning, for that has dropped away now that the "new age" in the Spirit has come.

Reformed Baptists are not alone in recognising that in the New Testament era a change such as we have described has taken place. Many Paedobaptists, when they are not defending infant baptism, have no problem in recognising it. G. Ernest Wright says, "In the Old Testament the prophets pointed to the one Israel within the nation, whereas in the New Testament by a logical extension Israel became the 'seed of Abraham' by *faith* rather than heredity".[5]

Reformed Baptists welcome such an understanding of the relationship between the Testaments because it accords with their own. They would, however, plead with their fellow Reformed Christians in churches which practise infant baptism to apply this particular insight in a more thoroughgoing fashion than they do at present. In particular they would ask that they weigh the force of Paul King Jewett's argument, "Now if, in the typical age of the Old Testament, all the seed of Abraham is to be circumcised, even though they be of the 'circumcision only', then in the age of fulfilment, all those who answer to the type as the true seed of Abraham shall be baptised. And who are they? The New Testament gives an unequivocal answer. Those who are of *faith*, these are the sons of Abraham (Gal. 3: 7). Therefore, those who are of faith are to be baptised, which is just believers' baptism".[6]

Jewett's argument, though it falls strangely upon the ears of present-day Arminian-Dispensational Baptists who posit an extreme dichotomy between the Testaments, is not new, as he himself recognises. It has been part of the armoury of the Reformed Baptist apologist for a very long time. For example, Abraham Booth said:

> The different state of things under the old and new economy, and the apostle's distinction between the carnal and the spiritual seed of Abraham, being duly considered, the argument from analogy will run thus: As, under the old covenant, circumcision belonged to all the *natural* male descendants of Abraham; so, under the new covenant, baptism belongs to all the *spiritual* seed of Abraham, who are known to be such only by a credible profession of repentance and faith.[7]

This quotation shows what neither Arminian-Dispensational Baptists nor Reformed Paedobaptists seem to recognise, that there is a persistent stream of apologetic which is both Baptist and Reformed in its theological orientation. Those who maintain this apologetic today would ask both these other sections of fellow believers to realise that it is possible to be both Baptist and Reformed.

The Implications of the New Testament Interpretation of the Covenant

The New Testament interpretation of the Abrahamic covenant has very far-reaching implications, both for the theology and the practice of the church. Notice the order in which I put them. Our theology must go into our practice and our practice must be determined by our theology if we would be biblical Baptists.

(i) In respect of the doctrine of salvation, the New Testament interpretation of the covenant with Abraham commits us to a theology of divine grace, a grace which initiates, effects and perfects the salvation of God's elect. As Reformed Baptists we believe with all our hearts in *covenant* grace, that is, grace that really is grace since it is grace sovereignly administered through the covenant, in which God has pledged himself to be the God of his elect.[8] This being so, we heartily repudiate that charge our Reformed Paedobaptist brethren frequently bring against us, namely, that in insisting upon the necessity of repentance and faith as the conditions on which we baptise, we are guilty of subjectivism, of emphasising human decision to the neglect of prevenient grace.[9] Reformed Paedobaptists may, if they so choose, bring their charge against Arminian Baptists who emphasise free will; they may not, without making theological fools of themselves, lay such a charge at the door of Calvinistic Baptists. However, we must insist that the issue is not to be decided by opting for one or other of the terms of the antithesis, the objectivity of divine grace *or* the subjectivity of human decision; rather, there is need to appreciate that *both* the objective and subjective elements of the New Testament doctrine of salvation must be taken into account. On the one hand the New Testament is emphatic that the salvation of sinners is gloriously objective because it is grounded in the grace and favour of an unchanging God. It is wrought out because of an eternal covenant of redemption between the persons of the blessed Trinity to save elect sinners. It is in no way procured by man, it is altogether of grace. The chain of grace stretches from eternity to eternity, through time, to encircle the elect sinner. It is as certain that we shall be glorified as that we are already, by grace, justified. So certain then is this objective salvation that Paul can speak of glorification as

56

already having been accomplished (by using a past tense) when in fact it still awaits us (Rom. 8: 29-30).

Yet because we believe this we dare not, on the other hand, overlook the New Testament demand for repentance and faith as being necessary to our experiencing the benefits of redemption. "Repent and believe the Gospel" inevitably involves the subjective apprehension of the provisions of God's grace in Christ Jesus. We must, however, emphasise to our Reformed brethren that the subjectivity of which we are speaking rests upon God's grace, not upon man's free will or human decision. Repentance and faith, whilst exercised by human subjects, are not human products; they are both alike the gifts of a gracious God to his children. Our Saviour, we are expressly told, has been exalted to God's right hand on high to give repentance to his own,[10] and faith itself is the very gift of God.[11]

(ii) In respect of the doctrine of the church, the New Testament interpretation of the covenant with Abraham commits us to a view of the church which, while not perfectionist, takes with the utmost seriousness the New Testament concept of the church as the true Israel of God (Gal. 6: 16; Rom. 9: 7-8). We believe that if we are to be faithful to the New Testament doctrine of the church we must frame our definition of its visible membership, not in the light of its existing state which may be far from satisfactory, but in the light of the fact that it is, according to the New Testament, the body of Christ, the fellowship of the saints, the true Israel and the true circumcision.

Because we insist that as far as is humanly possible, the membership of the visible church should be composed of only those who give credible evidence of faith in Christ, we are frequently charged with being perfectionists who hold the impossible ideal of an absolutely pure church. We are accused of being Donatists, unrealistic and indeed hard-hearted and censorious Puritans.[12] But such charges are not in order as I must now show. In fact the disagreement between Reformed Baptists and *some* Reformed Paedobaptists *at this point* is not as wide as is so often suggested. Bannerman, when marking off the distinctions to be observed between the church invisible and the church visible represents the traditional Reformed position when he says, "The church invisible stands with respect to its members in an inward and spiritual relationship to Christ, whereas the church visible stands to him in an outward relationship only".[13] However, Professor John Murray has more recently shown, both in his book *Christian Baptism*[14] and in his address to the Banner of Truth Conference at Leicester, England, in July 1964, on "The Nature, Unity and Government of the Church",[15] that the New Testament describes the visible church as being in an *inward* relationship to Christ (whereas Bannerman predicted this only of the invisible church of God's elect). This fact comes to the clearest expression in Paul's description of the visible church at Corinth, which we should remember contained immoral persons. He describes that church "as sanctified in Christ Jesus, called to be saints" (1 Cor. 1: 2). He does not deny the essential nature of the Corinthian church as a community in Christ by adoptive grace merely because of the presence in it of some who ought not to be in membership at all. Indeed he expressly links this community, with all its problems (which might seem to make it less than a church in the New Testament sense), with the whole church visible—"saints, with all that in every place call upon the name of Jesus Christ our Lord, both theirs and ours". It is obvious that a Reformed Baptist finds himself in closer agreement with Professor Murray than with James Bannerman. My complaint is that the Professor does not argue to the obvious conclusion and become a Baptist, for he has accepted the Baptist doctrine of the visible church.

If we regard the visible church as vitally united to Christ (as it is in the New Testament) we have to adopt a certain theological method. We must not reason from what may be the present state of the church, of its being a mixed community of believers and unbelievers, and seek therefore to include *this situation* in our definition of the church. Instead we must work from the New Testament definition of the visible church as a fellowship of saints and apply its teaching to the existential situation. This surely is the only correct approach. Even though the leadership of churches is not infallible, and so false professors may at times be admitted into fellowship, nonetheless, it must strive for the purity of the visible church both in doctrine and in life. It is here I feel that Reformed Paedobaptists have unwittingly allowed their doctrine of the church to be shaped by existential considerations. They have tried to find a place within their view of the nature of the visible church for its admitted and recognised impurity, to which of course the practice of indiscriminate baptism has contributed.

The difference of approach which we have noticed can be illustrated by comparing the Westminster Confession of Faith (Chap. XXV, section v) with the Particular Baptist Confession of 1677 (sometimes called the 1689 Confession because of its wide publication in 1689) which is largely based upon the former. Both agree that "the purest churches under heaven are subject both to mixture and error and some have so degenerated as to become no churches of Christ, but synagogues of Satan", but what is significant is that the Scripture proofs offered are different. In proof that even the purest churches are subject to both mixture and error, the Westminster Confession points us to 1 Cor. 13: 12 and Matt. 13: 24-30. A reference to Rev. 2 and 3 is put in square brackets, presumably because this reference is regarded as being of secondary importance, or because it was added later. The 1677 Particular Baptist Confession appeals, interestingly enough, to 1 Cor. 15 (it has in mind presumably the heretical view of the resurrection of the body) and Rev. 2 and 3. What is so interesting is the absence from the Baptist Confession of any reference to the parable of the wheat and the tares (Matt. 13: 24-30). This omission is of the greatest significance. Although the authors of the 1677 Confession were prepared to concur with the authors of the Westminster Confession that "the purest churches under heaven are subject both to mixture and error", they were not prepared to apply the parable of the wheat and tares to the visible church, precisely because it appeared to them to sanction *a definition of the church as she had become, rather than of the church as she should be.*[16] It is a remarkable fact that Baptists have consistently refused to apply this parable to the visible church, whereas Reformed Christians of other ecclesiastical communions have had no hesitation whatsoever in so doing. I want to emphasise this point as strongly as possible, because it seems to me that we have two different conceptions of the visible church here, even when there is agreement on the fact that all visible churches are imperfect. The conception found in the Westminster Confession would appear to come to terms with the visible church as it is, whereas the 1677 Confession refuses to do this. Why is this? Is it because the Reformed theologians have to recognise the presence of considerable numbers of unconverted members in their churches who have not improved, as they say, upon their baptism? Is it that, recognising this fact, they have been forced to shape their definition of the visible church accordingly? It will not do to make the

59

counter-charge which is often made, that Baptists are perfectionists, for the 1677 Confession expressly denies this. Clearly this divergence is of the utmost practical importance. Imagine a visible church in which, among the office-bearers (say, the elders) these two different conceptions of the nature of the church are to be found. The one party would be prepared to be accommodating in regard to membership requirements, the other would not. Is not the melancholy story of Jonathan Edwards' rupture with the church at Northampton, Massachusetts, a warning to us of what happens when these two concepts come into conflict?[17] If I may say so in all charity, Reformed Baptists find it very hard to understand the willingness of some of their non-Baptist Reformed brethren to accept, as apparently normal, the state of the visible church as it is found today. They do not pretend that all is well with them, but they do believe that the situation must not be accepted as normal but reformed by the Word of God. So much, then, for the implications of the New Testament interpretation of the covenant.

The Strength of our Position

Finally, I come to the strength of our position. I believe that it is high time that we, as Reformed Baptists, stopped being defensive and apologetic, and ceased to be overawed by the weighty tomes of Paedobaptistic theology that have recently been re-issued, to the profit of us all in many respects. It is my conviction that ours is a position of great strength and consistency, precisely because it is consonant with the totality of the Scriptural doctrine of the church.

Firstly, we have a proper view of the relation between circumcision and baptism. Since I have already dealt with this point I want to do no more than give one quotation from C. H. Spurgeon's sermon on *Consecration to God Illustrated by Abraham's Circumcision*. "It is often said that the ordinance of baptism is analogous to the ordinance of circumcision. I will not contravert that point although the statement may be questioned. Supposing it be, let me urge on every believer here to see to it that in his own soul he realises the spiritual meaning both of circumcision and baptism and then consider the outward rites. For the thing specified is vastly more important than the sign. 'Well,' saith one, 'a difficulty suggests itself as to your views for an argument is often drawn from this fact that inasmuch as Abraham must circumcise all his seed,

60

we ought to baptise all our children.' Now observe the type and interpret it not according to prejudice but according to Scripture—in the type the seed of Abraham is circumcised—you draw the inference that all typified by the seed of Abraham ought to be baptised, and I do not cavil at the conclusion, but I ask you, who are the true seed of Abraham? Paul answers in Rom. 4: 8, 'They which are the children of the flesh, these are not the children of God; but the children of the promise are counted for the seed'. As many as believe on the Lord Jesus Christ, whether they be Jews or Gentiles, are Abraham's seed. Whether eight days old in grace, or more or less, everyone of Abraham's seed has a right to Baptism, but I deny that the unregenerate whether children or adults are of the spiritual seed of Abraham. The Lord will, we trust, call many of them by his grace, but as yet they are heirs of wrath even as others. At such times as the Spirit of God shall sow the good seed in their hearts they are of Abraham's believing seed, but they are not so while they live in ungodliness and unbelief, or are yet incapable of faith and repentance. The answering person in type to the seed of Abraham is, by the confession of everybody, the believer. And the believer ought, seeing that he is buried with Christ spiritually, to avow that fact by his public baptism in water according to the Saviour's own precept and example."[18]

Secondly, we can do justice to both the continuity and the diversity of redemptive revelation. We take seriously the one covenant of grace, yet we also do justice to the newness of the New Covenant, which when implemented has an inwardness which contrasts with the external aspects of the national adoption of Israel (Jer. 31: 13). All members of the church, as was not the case in Israel, are required to know the Lord and to have his law written on their hearts (v. 33). As Reformed Baptists, we need not read the Old Testament into the New, nor the New into the Old in an illegitimate fashion. We can do justice to the continuity and diversity of redemptive revelation without imposing the New Testament doctrine of the church on the Old Testament history of covenantal administration or wrapping the garb of the Old Testament theocracy round the body of Christ.

Thirdly, we have a proper view of the family, the church and the state. God, according to Scripture, has ordained three institutions for the benefit and blessing of mankind. He has ordained the family, which arises from the creation-ordinance of marriage (Gen.

61

2: 21-25). He has ordained the state to order the life of sinful men, so that they might enjoy the blessings of living in an ordered society subject to law (Gen. 9: 5-6; Rom. 13: 1 ff.; 1 Pet. 2: 13-14). He has also ordained the church, a people for his exclusive possession (1 Pet. 2: 5, 6, 9, 10). We confuse neither the family nor the state with the church, as our Reformed Paedobaptist brethren so often do. The family is the unit of Christian nurture when the parents are Christians, but there is no hereditary right to salvation inherent in membership of a Christian home. The church, on the other hand, is not the spiritual side of one coin, of which the state is the other. We repudiate sacralism on biblical grounds, in favour of what Verduin calls compositism.[19] This is the view that membership of the church is open only to those citizens of the state who have been subjects of the effectual calling of God, and that citizenship and church membership are two utterly distinct things resting upon two completely distinct grounds. Natural birth secures the privileges of state citizenship, but it cannot secure membership in the visible church. The proper ground for this is regeneration by the Holy Spirit.[20] Because we hold these views of family, church and state, we believe neither in the church membership of covenant infants nor in state churches. We have the basis, if we are true to our position, for a proper distinction between the church and the family on the one hand, and the church and the state on the other.[21]

Fourthly, we have a biblical foundation for our instruction of children. A most instructive and illuminating book by Lewis Bevins Schenck, *The Presbyterian Doctrine of Children in the Covenant: An Historical Study of the Significance of Infant Baptism in the Presbyterian Church in America*[22] can serve to illustrate my theme. Schenck explains the historical doctrine of the Presbyterian Church concerning the significance of infant baptism. He demonstrates that the ground for baptising an infant is exactly the same as the ground for baptising an adult, namely, the assumption that he is regenerate. He quotes Dr. Abraham Kuyper as saying, "That it is tantamount to overthrowing the classic Calvinistic view of infant baptism to deny:

"1. That children of believers are to be considered as recipients of efficacious grace, and that in them the work of efficacious grace has already begun.

62

"2. That when dying before having attained to years of discretion, they can only be regarded as saved.

"Of course," he adds, "Calvinists never declared that these things were necessarily so. As they never permitted themselves to pronounce official judgment on the inward state of an adult, but left the judgment to God, so they have never usurped the right to pronounce on the absence or presence of spiritual life in infants. They only stated how God would have us *consider* such infants and this consideration based on the Divine Word made it imperative to look upon their infant children as elect and saved and treat them accordingly."[23] Children then, according to the classic doctrine of Presbyterianism, are baptised on the ground that being children of believers they are already in the covenant and ought therefore to be given the covenant sign of baptism.

This view of the child's status has, we should realise, important implications for Presbyterian pedagogics. *The child is to be treated and instructed, not as if it were an unbeliever, but on the assumption that it is already a child of God.* How this works out in practice is to be seen from a quotation which Schenck gives from a letter of Dr. J. W. Alexander written in March, 1845, complaining about the neglect of infant baptism by some Christian parents, in which he says, "But O! how we neglect that ordinance! *i.e.* treating children in the church just as if they were out of it. Ought we not daily to say (in its spirit) to our children—'You are Christian children— you are Christ's—you ought to think and feel and act as such!' And, on this plan carried out, might we not expect more early fruit of the grace than by keeping them always looking forward to a point of time at which they shall have new hearts and *join the church?* I am distressed with long-harboured misgivings on this point".[24] Schenck shows how the Great Awakening with its emphasis on the necessity of conversion challenged the whole Presbyterian theory of covenant-children. Indeed his third chapter is entitled, intriguingly enough, "The Threat of Revivalism to the Presbyterian Doctrine of Children in the Covenant". What happened was this. Many Christian parents, influenced by the Awakening, came to regard their children as in Adam, as under wrath and as not, therefore, in the covenant by birth. Hence they neglected to have them baptised as infants, preferring to wait till there was definite evidence in their lives of the fruits of conversion.

Jedediah Andrews, of Philadelphia, in a letter written to a friend in 1741, protested against the revival preachers' emphasis on the necessity of conversion and on the necessity of knowing that one was converted. "A prevailing rule to try converts," says Andrews, "is that if you don't know when you are without Christ and unconverted, etc., you have no interest in Christ, let your love and practice be what they may—which rule as it is unscriptural, I am of the mind, will cut off nine in ten if not ninety and nine in a hundred of the good people in the world that have had a pious education."[25] As a result of the effect of the revival a difference arose between the theologians of the Presbyterian Church in the States. On the one hand, Dabney, Thornwell and others, regarded baptism as making the child a child of the covenant. They held that by baptism the child is introduced by an "ecclesiastical covenant" into the visible church, but they did not advocate baptism on the classic ground that the infant is presumptively God's child by regeneration.[26] Such a child was, in their view, to be regarded as an unregenerate baptised child until it gave evidence of a new heart. Charles Hodge, on the other hand, took the classic view over against Thornwell and Dabney. He held that presumptive regeneration is the ground of infant baptism. Significantly he said, "We see not how this principle can be denied in its application to the church without giving up our whole doctrine and abandoning the ground to the Independents and Anabaptists".[27]

From Schenck's interesting book several vital points emerge:

1. Our view of children differs radically from that of Reformed Paedobaptists. We regard our children, I trust, as non-Christians, while they regard theirs as Christians, unless they take the position held by Thornwell and Dabney. If they take the latter view they are, as Hodge realised, half-way to becoming Baptists! There must be, therefore, a radically different approach to the child in both cases.

2. In principle, our instruction of children ought to destroy a sense of false security and hypocrisy. If we were to regard a child as already regenerate on the ground of heredity membership of the covenant, we would encourage him to entertain a false hope and also to exhibit an expected pattern of behaviour which appears to be consistent on the surface with his covenant status. We do not say to our children, "Be a good Christian child," but "Repent and believe the gospel".[28]

3. Our instruction of children does not encourage false sentimentality, indeed, it does the opposite. We take seriously the child's lost estate and alienation from the living God, and thus we can effectively apply the radical remedy of the Gospel. We find that Paedobaptist writings so often range between high and abstruse theology and the most maudlin sentimentality. Bannerman writes (and I speak with tenderness here, for I am not poking fun at him) of a Christian mother weeping at the open grave of her infant, and says that "it is an unspeakable consolation for her to know that the little one, whom she took from off her breast to lay in the tomb, was indeed signed with the sign of Christian Baptism".[29] How hard-hearted this quotation makes us Baptists appear to be! But, we ask, can such sentiments be justified by the Word of God? Charles Hodge is scarcely better. He says, "It is a great evil to be aliens from the commonwealth of Israel and strangers from the covenants of promise. Those parents sin grievously against the souls of their children who neglect to consecrate them to God in the ordinance of baptism". How a high Calvinist like Hodge could have written the following sentence is a mystery to me: "Do let the little ones have their names written in the Lamb's book of life, even if they afterwards choose to erase them; being thus enrolled may be the means of their salvation".[30]

Our attempt to understand covenant theology has not been, I trust, a mere academic and theoretical exercise. This matter is of vital importance to every area of church life of which we can think. Our doctrine of salvation and of the church, our evangelism and our view of children are all intimately related to the view we take of the Abrahamic covenant. If we misinterpret this, and especially if we misunderstand its New Testament significance, there will be profound consequences in all of these areas.

--- --- ---

NOTES

1. See my article, "The Argument from Silence in Reformed Paedobaptist Apologetic", *Reformation Today*, No. 3, Autumn 1970, pp. 6-9.
2. Dispensationalists maintain that the promise of a literal inheritance in the land of Canaan still holds good for the Jewish people. See J. D. Pentecost, *Things to Come*, Dunham, Grand Rapids, 1964, pp. 90-94.

Since dispensationalism is not usually found in Reformed circles it is not necessary to take it into consideration at this point.

3. J. B. Lightfoot, *The Epistle of St. Paul to the Galatians,* Zondervan reprint edition, Grand Rapids, 1965, p. 143.
4. Ralph P. Martin, *Colossians: The Church's Lord and the Christian's Liberty,* Paternoster Press, Exeter, 1972, p. 85 argues against G. R. Beasley-Murray, *op. cit.,* p. 153 ff., who takes "the circumcision of Christ" as referring to his death, that it means the spiritual renewal of the heart. I find myself convinced by Martin's arguments.
5. G. E. Wright, *The Biblical Doctrine of Man in Society,* S.C.M., London, 1954, p. 79.
6. Jewett, *op. cit.,* p. 419.
7. Abraham Booth, *Paedobaptism Examined,* p. 265, quoted Jewett, *op. cit.,* p. 420.
8. *e.g.* Gen. 17: 7; Heb. 11: 16; Rev. 21: 3.
9. If men are "dead in trespasses and sins" (Eph. 2: 1) then conversion in adulthood is no less the result of prevenient grace than conversion in childhood.
10. Acts 5: 31.
11. Eph. 2: 8.
12. See L. Verduin, *The Reformers and their Stepchildren,* Paternoster Press, Exeter, 1966.
13. Bannerman, *op. cit.,* Vol. 1, p. 39.
14. *Christian Baptism,* pp. 42-5.
15. Published by the Banner of Truth Trust, 1964.
16. For a helpful exposition of this parable see Alexander MacLaren, *Exposition of Holy Scripture, The Gospel According to St. Matthew,* chaps. IX-XVII, Hodder & Stoughton, n.d., pp. 234-43.
17. The church divided from Edwards over the issue as to who should be admitted to the Lord's Supper, Edwards contending that believers only should partake.
18. *Metropolitan Tabernacle Pulpit,* Passmore & Alabaster, London, 1868, XIV, pp. 695-6. Spurgeon's appendix on baptism to his edition of Thomas Watson's *Body of Divinity* has been recently published by Henry Walter, Worthing, under the title *Spurgeon on Baptism* (1972).
19. Verduin distinguishes between sacralism and compositism as follows: Sacralism sees the church as embracing all in a given territory whereas compositism views the church as "a community of experiential believers" (p. 17), an element *in* society, not society itself in its ecclesiastical expression.
20. See *e.g.* Phil. 3: 3; 1 Thess. 1: 4-6; Rom. 1: 7.
21. For a short treatment of the tragic results of the failure to distinguish properly between Church and State see H. M. Carson, *Riots and Religion,* Henry Walter, Worthing, 1970.
22. Yale University Press, 1940.
23. *ibid.,* quoted p. 18.
24. *ibid.,* quoted p. 81.
25. *ibid.,* quoted p. 71.
26. *ibid.,* p. 87. The classic position, held by Calvin (see Schenck, pp. 9-10) and most other Presbyterian theologians, is that children of believing parents are to be baptised on the grounds of their being included with their parents in the covenant of grace, not because baptism makes them children of an ecclesiastical covenant (see Dabney and Thornwell).

27. *ibid.,* quoted p. 99.
28. How sharply the Reformed Baptist position is marked off from the Reformed Paedobaptist position can be seen in Charles Hodge, *The Mode and Subjects of Baptism,* reprinted Belfast, 1966, pp. 41-3. "To our faith," writes Hodge, "the presumption should be that they are the Lord's, and that as they come to maturity they will develop a life of piety. Instead of waiting, therefore, for a period of definite conviction and conversion, we should rather look for, and endeavour to call out, from the commencement of moral action, the emotions and experiences of the *renewed* heart" (p. 42, my italics). How large a place infant baptism occupies in Hodge's pedagogics may be seen in the following statement: "Such a faith as this (*i.e.* that believes that the child of Christian parents is in the covenant of grace) is valuable beyond expression. It is fostered by the ordinance of baptism, without which it is not commonly formed" (p. 34). In other words, Baptists have neither the same confidence or desire that their children will be saved as Paedobaptists, a notion too absurd to necessitate refutation.
29. Bannerman, *op. cit.,* Vol 2, p. 121. There is a strange inconsistency in Bannerman's thinking. If the ground of infant baptism is presumptive regeneration because the child of Christian parents is included with them in the covenant of grace, then the consolation, should such an infant die, ought to reside not in the fact of his having received the sign of the covenant but in his interest in the covenant itself.
30. *Systematic Theology,* Vol. 3, p. 388. In the context Hodge would appear to be saying that baptism is the cause of election!

PART II

CHAPTER 5

CHILDREN IN THE OLD TESTAMENT

In recent years there has been a considerable ferment in Baptist circles in the United Kingdom, and to a lesser extent perhaps in the United States of America, over the question of the relationship of children of believing parents to the Church.

It would be true to say that to a very considerable extent this ferment has been generated by scholars *within* Baptist ranks whose ecumenical sympathies and contacts have forced them to examine afresh the issues of infant baptism and the status of children of believing parents. The concern of these scholars to work out a contemporary Baptist theology of children has found expression in a number of pamphlets, articles and books.[1]

As Reformed Baptists we, of course, have to do battle on more than one front. We have to deal with not only the views of non-Reformed and (in many cases) decidedly liberal Baptists, but also the attacks of our Reformed Paedobaptist brethren. As we have already noted, the latter feel that we have no theology of believers' children and that we fail to do justice in our teaching to the biblical concept of the covenant seed. We therefore recognise the need for a positive biblical theology of believers' children which will be faithful to the whole tenor of Scripture, and in particular to the Scriptural doctrine of the Church.

We will examine three aspects of the position of children in Old Testament Israel.

1. *Entry into the Covenant Community*

The unfolding of God's purpose of grace towards mankind, through the chosen people of Israel, began with the calling of Abram in Haran. Abram was addressed as an individual, but not as a mere individual, for involved in his response to the divine

68

command were Lot, Sarai, "and all their possessions which they had gathered, and the persons they had gotten in Haran" (Gen. 12: 5a). It seems likely that Abram's clan (for such it was rather than a family as we conceive of it today) included not only the children born of his large retinue of servants, but also the many slaves he had obtained by purchase. The fact that Abraham (as his name became) was able at a later date to muster from his own household 318 trained men to pursue the captors of Lot (Gen. 14: 14), demonstrates how large his clan group was. When God called Abram he called an individual who was the head of a very considerable authority structure which included his nephew, Lot, his wife, Sarai, any concubines he may have had and the families of his retainers and slaves.

As the head of the authority structure, Abram was responsible under God for ensuring that within his clan the stipulations of the covenant which God made with him (Gen. 17: 4 ff.) were faithfully kept. Of first importance in the covenant demands was the observance of the rite of circumcision (Gen. 17: 10 ff.). This rite was not practised at puberty, as it is in many cultures, but as soon as practicable after birth (v. 12). It was demanded only of males, a fact which indicates the strictly subordinate place of females within the covenant community of Israel.

The fact that circumcision was performed shortly after birth would suggest that the male child was regarded as a member of the covenant community by virtue of his birth. One was *born* into Israel by natural birth, which was perhaps why circumcision was performed on the organ of generation. Thus at no time was the Israelite child regarded as being outside the covenant community; there was in fact never a moment from his birth onwards when he would have been regarded as other than belonging to it. In this connection it is surely significant that the Old Testament knows of no ceremony subsequent to circumcision which like the "bar mitzvah" of Judaism marked the person as a full member of the covenant community.

It should be noted, however, that provision was made for exclusion from the covenant community. "Any uncircumcised male who is not circumcised in the flesh of his foreskin shall be cut off from his people: he has broken my covenant" (Gen. 17: 14 R.S.V.). However, failure to be circumcised was not the only reason for exclusion (see Deut. 21: 18-21; Lev. 17: 1-13).

It is often argued by Reformed Paedobaptists that whereas a child is to be included within the church by virtue of its birth connection with its believing parents, he or she may in riper years choose to repudiate the faith and thus contract out of the church. It is impossible to see that this argument can find support in the Old Testament, for the cutting off of an apostate person was on the ground that the covenant stipulations had been broken, and thus the death penalty had to be carried out. It would seem that as no provision was made for voluntary entry into the covenant community, so none was made for voluntary withdrawal. Rather, the transgressor was cut off, that is to say he was executed, and thus put outside the covenant people. Anthony Phillips is surely correct when he writes,

> "Once a man entered into the covenant relationship, then his children would be born into that relationship, *and were to have no opportunity of repudiating it.* One could never contract out of Yahwism. To do so amounted to a breach of the criminal law, to which one was automatically subject, and so led to execution."[2]

We must now summarise this section. Firstly, the male child entered the covenant community at birth, the covenant-sign being circumcision which was administered shortly after birth. Secondly, the male child seems to have been regarded as a full (albeit an immature) member of the covenant people from the moment of birth, since no further rite subsequent to circumcision was required. There is thus, we may notice, no Old Testament analogy for confirmation, as there undoubtedly is for baptism. Thirdly, whilst provision was made for exclusion from the covenant people, no allowance was made for voluntary withdrawal.

2. *Status within the Covenant Community*

What was the status of children, especially males, within the community? Quite obviously, they were not regarded as responsible adults, capable of making decisions. This can be inferred from the fact that whilst the Old Testament nowhere speaks of an age of accountability, as we sometimes do, it does recognise the difference between a child for whom decisions are made, and a person who makes decisions. For example, Isa. 7: 15-16 draws the distinction between the age before which "the *child* knows how to refuse the evil and choose the good", and afterwards. Jonah 4: 11, recognises, it would seem, the same distinction in stating that in Nineveh there are "more than a hundred and twenty thousand persons who do not know their right hand from their left".

Thus Israelite children were not regarded as responsible adults, nor could they be until they were heads of their own households, because an unmarried adult son would have remained in his father's household until marriage, and thus would have been under his authority. The children were nonetheless regarded as members of the covenant people in the full sense.

That male children were regarded as full members of the covenant community can be seen from the following evidence. Firstly, according to Exod. 23: 17 and Deut. 16: 16 *all* male members were commanded to appear before the Lord at the central shrine. The fact that no distinction is drawn between male children and male adults would suggest that male children were always regarded as full members of the covenant people. Secondly, it is assumed that children will be present at and participate in the celebration of the passover. "And when your *children* say to you, 'What do you mean by this service?' you shall say, 'It is the sacrifice of the Lord's passover . . .' " (Exod. 12: 26, 27; cf. Deut. 6: 20 ff.).

If our interpretation is correct then those who make much of the circumcision/baptism analogy should make a little more of the Passover/Lord's Supper analogy. If following circumcision infants were present at, and partook of the passover, then why do our Reformed Paedobaptist friends deny the Lord's Supper to infants? If the analogy holds good in the one instance it should do so in the other.

Jewett's comment on the matter is surely apposite,

"Having embraced their children in the covenant by giving them baptism, Paedobaptists then exclude them from that covenant by refusing them participation in the covenant meal."[3]

As soon as they were capable of understanding, children were to be instructed as to the covenant-redemptive action of God in history on behalf of his people, and they were to be taught the stipulations of the covenant law. The centre of religious instruction was neither the tabernacle nor the temple, but the home (Deut. 6: 7; Exod. 10: 2; 12: 26-27; Gen. 18: 19). As the head of the family the father was responsible for teaching his children, although often the mother would share in the task of instruction (Prov. 31: 1).

Attention is concentrated upon the instruction of sons in general but of the first-born son in particular, since he would, in the normal course of events, succeed his father and become responsible for upholding the covenant stipulations.

Thus whilst at no time was a child not a member of the covenant community, his subordinate status was evidenced by the fact that he was under instruction in the faith of Israel.

It is difficult to determine from the available evidence at what stage the child was regarded as being accountable for his actions. R. E. Clements argues, to my mind quite unconvincingly, that twenty *became* the age from which moral accountability was reckoned.[4] I say "became" because he regards Num. 14: 28-31, to which he appeals, as part of the so-called "P" document. In consequence (according to the usual critical dating of "P") it was only after the time of the exile that twenty became the accepted age of accountability.

Apart from the fact that on the surface, at least, the narrative has nothing to say about the origination of the age of accountability, twenty would seem to be an impossibly high figure. Marriage could be contracted at a much earlier age, and thus we are faced with the position that married Israelites under twenty years of age were regarded as not accountable for their actions!

In the teaching of the prophets Jeremiah and Ezekiel there is a greater stress upon individual responsibility than was previously the case in the history of Israel. Jeremiah denies that children are punished for their father's sin. In the days of the new covenant no longer will the popular saying be quoted:

"The fathers have eaten sour grapes, and the children's teeth are set on edge.
But every one shall die for *his own sin;* each man who eats sour grapes, his teeth shall be set on edge" (Jer. 31: 29, 30).

Ezekiel teaches the same truth. Starting with the statement that "the soul that sinneth it shall die" (18: 4) Ezekiel pictures three generations. The first man is righteous, and so he will live (18: 5-9). His son, however, is a robber and a shedder of blood. He would not live because he had a righteous father but rather ". . . shall surely die; his blood shall be upon himself" (18: 10-13). The grandson of the righteous, and the son of the wicked who "sees all

72

the sins which his father has done, and fears . . . he shall not die for his father's iniquity; he shall surely live" (18: 14-17).

Despite his stress upon individual responsibility, Ezekiel no-where attempts to define the age at which a child or youth becomes responsible before God, nor do any other of the Old Testament writers, so far as I am aware. What bearing this fact has upon the theology of children is not easy to determine.

Does the lack of any attempt to tie the concept of accountability to a particular age mean that accountability varies from individual to individual? It is hard to say "yes" or "no" to such a question. Does accountability vary according to responsibility? In the light of Ezek. 3: 16-21 I would suggest that it does. Ezekiel's position as "a watchman for the House of Israel" made him accountable to God for any failure to warn the wicked. Did the position of instructed children in Israel not render them even *more* accountable to God than the children of the heathen nations? Amos 3: 2 clearly indi-cates that it did.

We may conclude this part of the chapter by summarising the evidence thus far. Firstly, all the evidence suggests that children were regarded as full members of the covenant community from birth. They could not become members in any fuller sense after birth, since birth into an Israelite family (and circumcision in the case of a male child) placed them without equivocation in the covenant people of God. Secondly, male children participated in the worship of the tabernacle and in the observance of the passover. But thirdly, the subordinate status of the child (which was not inconsistent with full membership of the covenant people from birth) was recognised by the fact that he did not know the differ-ence between good and evil for some years after his birth, and also by the fact that he was under instruction in the faith of Israel.

It must be frankly admitted that the Old Testament does not tell us a great deal about children, probably because they were subordinate to the authority structure of the patriarchal family. There is so much more that we would like to know, but we have to respect the silence of the Old Testament. How, for example, was the nature of the child viewed? Though there are glimpses of a doctrine of original sin (*e.g.* Psa. 51: 5) they are glimpses, and no more.

Add to the paucity of evidence the problem of how to relate it to the New Testament teaching on the church and you begin to appreciate that the whole matter of the theology of children is one of the most difficult areas in biblical theology. A further strand of teaching that is often neglected when the Old Testament position on children is studied now needs consideration.

3. *The Remnant: Election within Election*

We have seen so far that the family was the sphere in which the covenant obligations and privileges were encountered. By being born into an Israelite family, or more precisely a clan, the male child entered, upon receiving the sign of circumcision, into the covenant community of Israel. The child was related to the covenant community through the clan or family.

However, in the darkening days of apostasy before and subsequent to the exile, we find that the concept of a remnant of people who are faithful to Jehovah amidst the general declension, comes into prominence.

In the earlier period of Israel's history there is little thought of the faithful remnant. The reason is obvious. As Henton Davies puts it, "The history of Israel from Moses to the monarchy is the history of the achievement of the idea and the fact of Israel".[5] During this period, therefore, one would not expect the idea of the remnant to occur. When the nation departs from God and becomes apostate, then the idea of the remnant reappears (we find the first trace of the concept in the story of Noah).

Davies continues his survey of the idea of the remnant,

"The fall of the northern Kingdom before the Assyrians in 722 B.C. leaves Judah as the remnant of Israel. In 2 Kings 17: 18 'and Jehovah was very angry with Israel, and removed them out of his sight; there was none left but the tribe of Judah only' (cf. 2 Kings 21: 14; Psa. 78 espec. vv. 67-8; Hos. 1: 7; Isa. 1: 8; 28: 5; Mic. 2: 12). Such passages show that Judah was regarded as the remnant of Israel. The prophetic denunciation of Judah leads us in turn to expect a further shrinking in the remnant. In this way begins to emerge the idea of a remnant of Judah (Isa. 4: 2 ff.; 37: 31, 32; Zeph. 2: 7; Jer. 40: 11, 15; Ezek. 11: 13; 14: 22; Obad. 17) though the remnant which survives the exile . . . is variously described (cf. Jer. 3: 11-14; 31: 2-9; Zech. 8: 6, 12; Ezra 9: 8, 13, 14, 15)."[6]

The story of the remnant is thus the history of a dwindling process, "From the first humanity to the family of Noah; from this second humanity to a family again, that of Abraham; from the nation of Abraham's descendants and related groups, that is Israel, to Judah, and still smaller groups".[7]

It is significant that Paedobaptists concentrate their attention on the early period of Israel's history. They point out that every male child was circumcised, and was regarded from birth as a member of the covenant community. But they tend to be silent on the later prophetic period, and especially with regard to the prophetic teaching concerning the remnant and spiritual circumcision.

Yet it is this later period which is of especial importance for the New Testament doctrine of the church. As Wheeler Robinson rightly points out, "the use of the doctrine of a righteous remnant . . . marks the future transference of religion from a nationalistic to an ecclesiastical basis".[8]

The emergence and development of the remnant concept had important implications for the family and the child. Quite obviously the basis of membership of the remnant is different from the basis of membership of the covenant people. In the latter case birth sufficed for membership, but in the former it did not. Those belonging to the remnant "trembled at the word", they were circumcised in heart, they did not bow the knee to Baal. In other words not natural but spiritual birth constituted them members of the remnant.

Obviously the child could be a member of the remnant only on the same basis as the adult, through being circumcised in heart. It is quite impossible to conceive of the child being included in the remnant simply because he or she was born into a family, the head of which was in fact a member of the faithful remnant. Neither was it a question of the child being regarded as a member of the remnant until he or she might decide to contract out by repudiating the faith of the head of the family. This would not have been possible because the faithful remnant, by definition, included only those who by the exercise of responsible faith and obedience had, as it were, contracted in!

The Old Testament teaching about the faithful remnant comes, of course, to its most pointed expression in the promise of the new covenant. The new covenant (Jer. 31: 32) is expressly distinguished from the old Sinaitic covenant in that it is to be written, not on tablets of stone, but upon the fleshy tables of the heart. The new covenant people were to be distinguished from the old in this respect: they shall all know the Lord (v. 34), "from the least of them unto the greatest of them".

Again, it is surely obvious that the promise of the new covenant brings about a change in the basis on which the godly can be members of the covenant people. After making every allowance for the spiritual import of circumcision it still remains true that membership of natural Israel was conditional upon natural birth, whereas membership of the new covenant people is dependent upon spiritual re-birth.

Both the concept of the remnant and the promise of the new covenant mark the transference of religion from a nationalistic to an ecclesiastical basis. So long as religion remained upon a nationalistic basis a child was related to the covenant people through birth into an Israelite family and by no other means. With the shift from a nationalistic to an ecclesiastical basis, a shift which begins to take place in the Old Testament but which is only completed in the New, the place of the child within the people of God undergoes a change.

The Old Testament nowhere states that a child cannot belong to the remnant. What is does imply, however, is that membership of the new covenant people cannot be on the basis of merely natural birth, but only on the basis of spiritual re-birth. Thus the election of the new covenant people within the national election of Israel, of the true Israel within Israel, brings about a change in the relation of children to the people of God.

If we would properly interpret the Old Testament teaching concerning children we must see the development of the history of the Old Testament revelation in its proper perspective. Firstly, we must not select the Mosaic period of revelation as if the last word about the church membership of children was said at that time. This is the error of Hodge's elaborate argument to prove that the basis of the church membership of children is the same now as it was in the Abrahamic and Mosaic periods of revelation.[9] Hodge writes as if the Old Testament revelation ceased with Moses; as if there were no teaching about a righteous remnant and the new covenant. One cannot simply draw a straight line from the Mosaic period to the New Testament, as the Pauline teaching in particular makes clear. Would Paul have written "they are not all Israel which are of Israel" (Rom. 9: 6) if the Old Testament had not contained unmistakable evidence that within the nation there was "a remnant according to the election of grace" (Rom. 11: 5)?

Secondly, as I have already argued, it is the Old Testament teaching about the remnant and the new covenant which raises the problem of re-defining the relationship of children to the covenant community. Not to recognise that re-definition is necessary, is to be unaware of the significance of the development of the Old Testament revelation. It is to stop at Sinai, and to refuse to go on to the prophets, who looked for the day when the promise of the new covenant would be actualised in the person of the covenant-surety, Jesus Christ himself.

NOTES

1. Of particular importance are the following:—
    (i) Articles:
    G. W. Rusling, "The Status of Children", *Baptist Quarterly*, Vol. XVIII, pp. 245-57.
    R. E. Clements, "The Relation of Children to the People of God in the Old Testament", *Baptist Quarterly*, Vol. XXI, pp. 195-205.
    G. R. Beasley-Murray, "Church and Child in the New Testament", *Baptist Quarterly*, Vol. XXI, pp. 206-18.
    M. J. Walker, "Baptist Theology of Infancy in the Seventeenth Century", *Baptist Quarterly*, Vol. XXI, pp. 242-62.
    W. Harrelson, "Children in the Church", *Foundations*, Vol. VI.
    (ii) Books or contributions to symposia:
    Neville Clark, "The Theology of Baptism", Chap. 8 in A. Gilmore (ed), *Christian Baptism*, Lutterworth Press, London, 1959.
    Alec Gilmore, *Baptism and Christian Unity*, Lutterworth Press, 1966. (See especially Chap. 6.)
    Clifford Ingle (ed), *Children and Conversion*, Broadman Press, 1970.
    (iii) Reports:
    The Child and the Church, Baptist Union of Great Britain and Ireland, 1966.
    The Gospel, the Child and the Church, Radlett Fellowship, 1967. A mimeographed reply to the above report.
2. Anthony Phillips, *Ancient Israel's Criminal Law*, Basil Blackwell, Oxford, 1970, p. 81 (my italics).
3. Jewett, *op. cit.*, p. 381.
4. R. E. Clements, *Baptist Quarterly*, Vol. XXI, pp. 197-8.
5. G. Henton Davies, article "Remnant" in Allan Richardson (ed), *A Theological Word Book of the Bible*, S.C.M., London, 1957, p. 190.
6. *ibid.*, p. 190.
7. *ibid.*, p. 190.

8. H. Wheeler Robinson, *Revelation and Inspiration in the Old Testament*, p. 157.

9. Charles Hodge, *Systematic Theology*, Vol. III, London and Edinburgh, 1873, pp. 546-59. Whilst Hodge points out that "circumcision was not the sign exclusively of the national covenant with the Hebrews ... because it was enjoined upon Abraham and continued in practice hundreds of years before the giving of the law on Mount Sinai, when the people were inaugurated as a nation" (p. 553), he fails to notice that in the course of the nation's history a remnant faithful to Jehovah came into increasing prominence. Had he done so he could hardly have written that "To suppose a man to be a Jew, and not at least a professed believer in these promises and predictions (of redemption), is a contradiction. A man, therefore, was a member of the Jewish commonwealth, only in virtue of his being a member of the Jewish Church; *at least, he could not be the former without being the latter*" (p. 553) (my italics). But it is precisely Hodge's identification of the Jewish nation with the Jewish Church that Paul denies in Rom. 2: 28-29.

Chapter 6

CHILDREN IN THE NEW TESTAMENT

As demonstrated in the previous chapter, even within the Old Testament itself there is a challenging of the assumption that merely natural descent from Abraham is sufficient to become a member of the true Israel of God. This assumption is further criticised in the teaching of John the Baptist, our Lord and the apostle Paul. It is true to say that their arguments exposing the false reasoning of the Judaism of their day provides much valuable material on the subject of children.

We find clear evidence in the preaching of John the Baptist that he challenged the reliance many Jews placed upon their physical descent from Abraham. Addressing himself to the Pharisees and Sadducees who came to be baptised he says, "And think not to say within yourselves, We have Abraham to our father: for I say unto you, that God is able of these stones to raise up children unto Abraham" (Matt. 3: 9). The Baptist's challenge occurs within the context of his call that they should "bring forth . . . fruits meet for repentance". It is obvious therefore that membership of the nation by virtue of natural birth is not regarded by John the Baptist as determinative for membership in the messianic community to be established by God's Son. God is able, in the exercise of his omnipotence, to raise up children unto Abraham. This statement implies that the natural sons of Abraham are not walking in the steps of Abraham's faith (Rom. 4: 12) and that God himself will raise true children to Abraham in fulfilment of his original promise. This conclusion is supported by the fact that John declares that the time of crisis has arrived, judgment has come to the nation: "And now also the axe is laid unto the root of the trees: therefore every tree which bringeth not forth good fruit is hewn down, and cast into the fire" (Matt. 3: 10).

In the teaching of our Lord we find criticism of the popular assumption that physical descent from Abraham sufficed to make a person a member of the true Israel of God. In John 8: 33 ff. our Lord confronts the scribes and the Pharisees (vv. 3, 13) who claim "We be Abraham's seed" (v. 33). In a somewhat ironic reply he says, "I know that ye are Abraham's seed; but ye seek to kill me, because my word hath no place in you" (v. 37). They certainly prove their merely *physical* descent from Abraham by wanting to murder the true Seed of Abraham, the Messiah. Quite rightly our Lord points out that, "If ye were Abraham's children, ye would do the works of Abraham" (v. 39), that is, they would do as Abraham did when he received God's word and carried out the things he commanded.

The apostle Paul carries the challenge even further when in Rom. 9 he argues that, from the very beginning of Israel's history, within the circle of those who had Abraham as their immediate progenitor, the mystery of divine election is to be seen. "For they are not all Israel, which are of Israel; neither, because they are the seed of Abraham, are they all children: but, in Isaac shall thy seed be called" (9: 6b-7).

Now it is against the background of this polemic against the popular assumption that merely physical birth made a man a member of the true covenant community that we must evaluate the New Testament teaching about children. It has been necessary to lay considerable emphasis upon the way in which the Baptist, our Lord and Paul argue because various writers, interpreting isolated statements about children out of harmony with this broader context, have made some texts teach that children of Christian parents are *by natural birth* to be counted as members of the covenant people of God. For example, J. Munro Gibson commenting on Matt. 19: 13-15 writes, "What a rebuke in these words of our Lord to those who deal with children indiscriminately, as if they were all dead in trespasses and sins. How it must grieve the Saviour's heart when lambs of his own fold who may have been his from their earliest infancy are taught that they are utterly lost, and must be lost for ever, unless they pass through some extraordinary change, which is to them only a nameless mystery. It is a mistake to think that children as a rule need to be dragged to the Saviour, or frightened into trusting him; what they need is to be *suffered* to come".[1]

Now the issue which Munro Gibson's exegesis raises is this: either the general and over-all teaching of the New Testament is

80

wrong, or his exposition of Matt. 19: 13-15 is incorrect. As we shall see later, his exegesis is astray. At this point it is worth noting some important implications of Munro Gibson's position, which is typical of that held by many Paedobaptists.

Firstly, if his understanding of Matt. 19: 13-15 (and other passages) is correct, then the New Testament polemic *against* the idea that natural descent from Abraham secures membership of God's people is quite unjustified. For, of what use is it to criticise such an idea if the same idea is allowed to reappear in the form "Children of Christian parents are to be accounted as members of the church"?

Secondly, the teaching of John the Baptist, our Lord and the apostle Paul on this subject, if it is valid, destroys the supposed parallel between the ground of membership in Israel and the ground of membership in the church. How could it do otherwise? Claiming Abraham as one's father without "bringing forth fruits meet for repentance" was condemned as carnal security which exposed one to the judgment of being "hewn down, and cast into the fire" (Matt. 3: 10) and to claim Christian parentage as a ground for membership in the church is nothing other than a reassertion of a principle which is explicitly condemned. There can be *no* parallel drawn between membership of national Israel and the church membership of infants which does not re-assert the principle of natural birth. Yet it is just this principle which is so consistently denied in the New Testament.

Thirdly, in Rom. 9: 6 ff. Paul's argument to establish the position that "they are not all Israel, which are of Israel", presupposes the impossibility of regarding the children of believing parents as Christian children. Both Ishmael and Isaac had Abraham as their father, but only Isaac was the child of promise and was thus accounted as the true seed of Abraham (v. 8). It will not do to reply that the case of Ishmael was exceptional. Certainly Abraham, in response to his wife's promptings, resorted to carnal expediency in order to obtain an heir, but in the case of Esau and Jacob, in which there is no question of carnal expediency, the mystery of divine election is seen in the choice of Jacob and the rejection of Esau. It is abundantly clear that Paul did not regard the Old Testament as teaching that *all* the infant seed of believers were to be counted as children of promise. Nor, incidentally, did Paul think in terms of Esau contracting out of the covenant obligations, for he was aware that he was rejected before birth, not "having done any good or evil, that the purpose of God according to election might stand, not of works but of him that calleth" (Rom. 9: 11).

Having surveyed the background to the New Testament teaching about children we must now consider some passages dealing specifically with the subject.

(i) *Children in the teaching of our Lord*

Our Lord's teaching on the subject of children is contained in two passages: Matt. 18: 1-6 (parallels Mark 9: 33-37 and Luke 9: 46-48) and Matt. 19: 13-15 (Mark 10: 13-16 and Luke 18: 15-17). There is a difference in the setting in Matthew, for whereas in Mark's version our Lord asks the disciples what they are disputing about, in Matthew's account the disciples come to Jesus and ask "Who is the greatest in the kingdom of heaven?" Whatever the reason for the difference, the main point is clear that the issue among the disciples was the matter of precedence in the kingdom of God. To demonstrate the folly of their dispute, indeed the blindness in spiritual things which lay behind it, our Lord called a child to himself, and placed him (or her) in the midst of his disciples, telling them that unless they were converted and became as little children they could not enter the kingdom. To be the greatest they must humble themselves like this child.

Now the passage contains three problems of interpretation. Firstly, what is being commended to the disciples? Is it some virtue in children, such as humility, which is worthy of their imitation? Or is it less a virtue of character and more the humble dependence which arises from the child's position in an adult world which is in view? Secondly, has the expression "little ones who believe in me" reference to children alone, or does it mean disciples of Christ generally? Thirdly, what is the meaning of the statement that in heaven the angels of the little ones always behold the face of the Father (v. 10)?

Firstly, let us consider what is being commended. Many commentators assume that our Lord is commending the humility of children to his disciples. This type of interpretation would appear to find some support in the text, for verse four reads, "Whoever humbles himself like this child, he is the greatest in the kingdom". Furthermore, the general context of the incident could be held to support this understanding of the lesson being inculcated, for the

82

dispute was about the order of precedence in the kingdom of God, and true humility is content with the lowliest place. If this interpretation is correct then the conclusion follows that children generally exhibit the virtue of humility, whereas adults do not, but need to do so. According to this view, at some point or another, as children mature, they become selfish and aggressive over maintaining their status.

Despite the popularity of this type of interpretation it is very questionable whether it is justified. As Warfield points out, children are in any case not notable for humility! Our Lord himself was aware of this as he shows in his parable of the playing children (Matt. 11: 16-17). Another fact which tells against this interpretation is that our Lord does not call for the imitation of the virtue of humility but for conversion, which can be effected only by divine grace. In verse 3 the verb *straphēte* is passive, *"Except you be converted . . .".* The emphasis is not upon imitation, which is within human power to affect, but upon conversion, which can be brought about only by the power of divine grace. As Tasker points out the *kai* (and) is consequential, *"and* so become as little children".[2]

It seems to me that Tasker is quite correct when he writes, "Jesus is not saying here that children are outstanding examples of humility, or any other virtue. He is pointing out that arrogant men and women can only possess the humility necessary for entrance into the kingdom of heaven if they are prepared to be insignificant as little children were in the ancient world".[3]

In the ancient world the child occupied the lowliest and most obscure place in society. The child was utterly dependent upon the favour of its parents or guardians. Therefore, in setting a child in the midst of his disciples our Lord forcefully taught them that the type of utter dependence exhibited by the child's *position* is absolutely essential, for both entrance into, and greatness within the kingdom.

If this latter interpretation is correct, as I believe it is, then certain conclusions follow. Firstly, this passage cannot be used to support the idea that a child has certain spiritual qualities which adults ought to imitate. If pressed, such an idea becomes a virtual denial of the doctrine of original sin. Secondly, the passage does not lend support to the belief that all children, as children, are within the kingdom of God. The particular child is symbolic of the position of complete dependence, not of all children in general. The fourth verse bears this out, "Whosoever therefore shall humble himself as *this* little child", the particular child who came to Jesus when called. Neither does the third verse lend support to the notion that all children are within the kingdom of God since the phrase "become as children" cannot be made to mean that all children, as children, are within God's kingdom. Rather the Greek *hōs paidion* (*this* child) points to the need of conversion. One can compare here the conversion terminology of Judaism. A proselyte to Judaism was said on his baptism to have become "like a little child".[4]

Secondly, we must look at the reference of the phrase, "little ones which believe in me" (v. 6). Most commentators are agreed that the phrase refers to a wider company than children. As Warfield points out,[5] children are never called "little ones" in the Hebrew Old Testament. Furthermore, *mikroi* never occurs in the Septuagint (Greek translation of Old Testament) as a translation of any Hebrew word meaning children. The phrase does, however, have an Old Testament source, for Zech. 13: 7 refers to the little ones of the flock. In the Gospels the disciples are referred to as "little ones" (Matt. 10: 42; Mark 9: 42). They are also described as "children" (Mark 10: 24 *tekna*; Matt. 11: 25 *nēpiois*=Luke 10: 21, *i.e.* infant).

In the light of this evidence it seems that the phrase "little ones" is not restricted in meaning to children. It should be emphasised, however, that the general context makes it clear that it does include children, but not all children generally, for the text specifically says "little ones who *believe* in me". Again, careful exegesis demonstrates that this passage at least, provides us with no warrant for concluding that all children, as children, are included within the kingdom of God.

Thirdly, we come to a consideration of the difficult statement that "in heaven their angels do always behold the face of my Father which is in heaven" (Matt. 18: 10).

That angels do exercise a protective function as part of their ministry is abundantly clear from Scripture (*e.g.* Gen. 19: 15, 16; Heb. 1: 14). What Jesus is saying is that "little ones who believe in him" are especially the objects of his Father's care through the ministry of angels.

Matt. 19: 13-15 does not need such detailed consideration as

Matt. 18: 1-6, because it raises only one major problem of interpretation and that is the meaning of the phrase translated in the Authorised Version, "for of such is the kingdom of heaven" (v. 14).

The Greek is ambiguous. It may mean "belongs to" or "consists of". Quite clearly the context demands that it is children who are in view in this statement. Luke employs *brephos* instead of *paidia*, making it clear that the children were babes in arms. The Greek can therefore mean that the kingdom of heaven belongs to children such as those brought to Jesus or, more unlikely, that it consists of such children.

Again we have to face the question of whether our Lord means children as such, or children as a symbol of a certain status or attitude. *Toioutos*, translated "of such" is a correlative adjective meaning "of such a kind, such as this". When used with a noun and with the article, as here, it is usually attributive, meaning "one child like this".

As early as Origen and Jerome[6] it was argued that Jesus did not say, "Suffer the children to come to me, for to these (*toutōn*) belongs the kingdom", but, "to such as these (*toiouton*) belongs the kingdom". This interpretation, as Beasley-Murray points out, has been advocated by some weighty names (Plummer, Dalman, J. Weiss, J. Schmid, R. E. O. White), but as another Murray (John) has demonstrated it cannot be sustained.

Certainly it is true that the same saying in Mark's version occurs in conjunction with the statement "Whosoever shall not receive the kingdom of God as a little child, he shall not enter therein" and thus sanctions the idea that the kingdom belongs to all those who believe in Christ and his message with childlike faith. But the question is, does the interpretation, the kingdom belongs to the childlike, exhaust the meaning intended by our Lord? Is the thought here of literal children? Some think not. For example R. E. O. White writes:

"As we have seen, Jesus constantly addressed himself to the reason and conscience of adults, and so ought his followers. All three evangelists, on the evidence just given, plainly take the words to mean 'of such as children is the kingdom of heaven'— the kingdom belongs to the *childlike*. Nothing is said of the relation of the child himself to the kingdom and to eternal life; but the incident is another priceless illustration of Jesus' attitude of love and gentleness, goodwill and prayerfulness, toward the child."[7]

The difficulty with this view is that it ignores the force of the conjunction "for" or "because" (*gar*). It is a straining of language to make our Lord mean: "Let the children come to me, *for* the kingdom belongs to people who are like them, people who exhibit a childlike spirit". This is the more so since *toioutōs* (of such as these) by no means implies the exclusion, but rather the inclusion of the one mentioned. The child is one of the class it represents. When the Jews cried out against Paul (Acts 22: 22) "Away with such an one!" (*toiouton*) they did not mean away with someone like Paul, but rather, away with Paul and everyone like him (cf. Heb. 7: 26 which says "For such (*toioutos*) an high priest became us" referring to our Lord, who is unique). In the light of these examples our Lord must mean that the kingdom belongs to these children and all others like them.[8]

Before our Paedobaptist friends rejoice with great glee in what appears to be a capitulation to their position, it must be pointed out that there is not a word in the passage which would oblige us to restrict our Lord's statement to "covenant" children. He does not say that to covenant children belongs the kingdom of God, but to children without distinction. If all children are in view, and if infant baptism can be got out of this passage (which it can, only if it is first read in!) then the text justifies the indiscriminate baptism of all infants, not the restriction of infant baptism to the children of believing parents.

Now in what sense are children to be regarded as belonging to the kingdom? The parallel passage in Mark 10: 13-16 will help us to arrive at the answer. Verse 15 declares the necessity of receiving the good news of the kingdom of God *as a child receives it*. The previous verse provides "a supreme illustration of children receiving the good news; they come to the Saviour with a love and trust answering to his love".[9] Here it is not the passivity of children, but their receptivity, which is in view. When Jesus called, the children came and threw themselves into his arms to be blessed. So to come in faith to him is to become an heir of the kingdom. Thus these children, and all children like them, form a picture of the ideal human response to the Lord's invitation in the Gospel.

This saying, of course, provides no warrant for the popular idea that children are born into the kingdom of God. As Beasley-Murray[10] points out, the sayings in Matt. 19: 4, Mark 10: 14 and Luke 18: 16 share the same form as the Beatitudes in Matt. 5: 3, 10, "theirs is the kingdom of heaven", *i.e.* they will inherit the kingdom of heaven at the end of the times. Children are thus said to be the destined heirs of the kingdom. They are to be allowed access to Jesus, for the kingdom of heaven will be given to just such at the Judgment and glory of the appearing of Christ. On what grounds? By virtue of their coming to Jesus (Mark 10: 14) and receiving the word of the kingdom (Mark 10: 15).

This interpretation does not necessitate imputing to the text notions of the supposed sinlessness or non-accountability of children, nor the concept of their membership, by birth, of the people of the covenant, nor the idea that they are covered by the redemptive work of Christ. What our Lord was establishing in the minds of his disciples was that children should not be denied access to himself, and the fact that children can and do, in terms of their own experience and understanding, come to Christ.[11]

It now remains to summarise our Lord's teaching on the subject of children. Firstly, in neither Matt. 18: 1-6 nor 19: 13-15 does he teach that children as a whole are within the kingdom of God on the ground of supposed innocence or non-accountability. Children belong to the kingdom of God only if in simple trust, they come to Christ.

Secondly, it is evident that our Lord had a tender regard for children, and taught that his Father in heaven had too. If he does not teach that all children, as children, are within the kingdom of God neither does he, on the other hand, teach that a child cannot enter into the kingdom. If utter dependence and open-hearted receptivity are pleasing to God, we cannot say that children are incapable of such. We can say only that God is able to work in, and on, whom he will, and therefore we dare not attempt to set a lower age limit for entry into the kingdom.

Thirdly, there is no warrant in our Lord's teaching for drawing a distinction between the children of believers and those of unbelievers. There is not a trace of the concept of covenant children in the two passages we have considered. The child he placed in the midst of his disciples is a symbol *as a child,* not as the child of believing parents. Neither does the second passage give us a warrant for the baptism of believers' children, as Tasker candidly admits.[12] If it did, it would provide a basis for the indiscriminate baptism of the children of all who desired, however vaguely, that Christ should bless their infants.

(ii) *Children in the rest of the New Testament*

I intend to look briefly at the place of children in the New Testament church, and then to consider two favourite passages in Paedobaptist apologetic, namely Acts 2: 39 and 1 Cor. 7: 14.

Much is sometimes made of the fact that Paul in his epistles, on occasions, addresses himself to children. For example, he addresses the Colossian believers as "saints and faithful brethren in Christ" (Col. 1: 2), and subsequently he admonishes children to obey their parents "in all things: for this is well pleasing unto the Lord" (Col. 3: 20). In Eph. 6: 1 he exhorts children to obey their "parents in the Lord: for this is right". The assumption is made that, in order to be so addressed, these children must have been members of the church, baptised as infants.

Aside from the fact that no Baptist preacher would have any difficulty in so admonishing the children in his congregation, it hardly follows that a child needs to be baptised before he can be admonished![13] Moreover, it could equally well be argued that the children Paul addresses had been already converted and so had been baptised as believers. The Paedobaptist Windisch allows this possibility, for he observes that the admonition to reverence parents (Col. 3: 20) implies the new obedience to the Gospel which delivers from the bondage of sin (Rom. 6: 17) rather than baptism in infancy.[14]

We consider now Acts 2: 39 (the promise is to you and to your children and to all that are afar off), which is hailed by Alford as "a providential recognition of Infant Baptism at the very founding of the Christian Church".[15] Attention to the context of this promise, however, demonstrates the implausibility of Alford's claim. In the first place, the promise of the Spirit includes the pledge that "your sons and your daughters shall prophesy, and your young men shall see visions" (Acts 2: 17), which hardly applies to infants. In the second place, the promise of verse 39 turns upon the phrase "even as many as the Lord our God shall call". Paedobaptists commonly distinguish between the children mentioned, regarding them as covenant children, and those who are afar off, *i.e.* born "out of covenant". This latter group alone must, they claim, be called to repentance and faith in order to be baptised. But if one thing is clear it is this; the last phrase of the verse, concerning God's call, governs all the preceding phrases. The promise is not only to those who respond on the day of Pentecost, but also to their descendants (children) and to those who are either outside the circle of Judaism or are beyond the confines of the land of Israel—to as many of any of these groups as God will call. What that call involves is plain to see, the inward work of the Spirit who enlightens the mind and renews the heart ("they were pricked in their heart" v. 37), and the response to that call ("what shall we do?" v. 37) after which one is baptised into the name of him who is freely offered in the gospel. Plainly the mention of children in this context provides no warrant whatever for infant baptism.

Finally, we must consider 1 Cor. 7: 14, a text so beloved of our Paedobaptist friends that the water of baptism gushes forth from it like the rock which Moses struck in the wilderness! Before we are swept away in the flood, however, we do well to note that at best Paul's statement could have only an *indirect* bearing on the question of whether the children of believers ought to be baptised. Paul is dealing here, not with the issue of a child's fitness for baptism, but with a marriage which has become divided through the reception of the Gospel by one partner (v. 11). Paul's advice is that, so long as the unbelieving partner is willing to continue in the married state, there is to be no separation on the part of the believer.

The basis on which the marriage should continue is indicated in verse 14. There is no defilement contracted by the believing partner or by the children, rather both the unbelieving partner and the children are "sanctified" by the believing partner.

In what sense are the children sanctified? According to Paedobaptists, not in the sense that they are "actually and inwardly holy persons, but that only having one Christian parent is enough to change their presumptive relations to God, enough to make them Christian children as distinguished from the children of unbelievers".[16]

This argument, however, proves too much, for the unbelieving husband is also said to be holy through the sanctifying of the believing wife. Should he not then be baptised also, as a holy unbeliever? No, say our Paedobaptist friends, for his "holiness" is so far different from the holiness of the children that it affords no ground for baptism. To maintain this position it is alleged that there is all the difference in the world between the verb *hēgiastai* and the adjective *hagioi*, but a glance at any lexicon will show the falsity of this. The root meaning of *hagios* is "God consecrated", *i.e. hēgiasmenos*. Indeed, for Paul in this very epistle *hēgiasmenoi* is a synonym for *hagioi* as 1: 2 makes clear, "Paul . . . to the church of God in Corinth, consecrated *hēgiasmenois* in Christ, called to be (members of the) consecrated people *hagiois* . . .". So if children are to be baptised on the strength of this verse, so also are sanctified unbelievers!

If we recognise that Paul is here employing the concept of ritual holiness found in the Old Testament we have the clue to the interpretation of 1 Cor. 7: 14. "For if the firstfruit be holy, the lump is also holy: and if the root be holy, so are the branches (Rom. 11: 16). In the first clause Paul echoes Num. 15: 21, "Of the first of your dough we shall give unto the Lord an heave offering", and by this act of offering the whole mass was consecrated or set apart. So in a marriage of which only one partner is a Christian, the offering up of the believing spouse sanctifies the whole, not in the sense of making inwardly holy but in setting the family apart for the operation of the grace of God in salvation through the witness of the believing partner (1 Cor. 7: 16). Paul is confident of the power of the Gospel to exert, in many cases, a truly converting and sanctifying influence on the family through a Christian father or mother. Therefore, the believer should on his part not break the marriage bond if the unbelieving partner is willing to continue in it.[17]

Positively 1 Cor. 7: 14 does allow us to state that, even where there is only one believing partner in a marriage, the children who are born are in a state of privilege, for they come under the sanctifying influence of the Gospel, but being in a state of privilege does not furnish a proper ground for baptism.

It remains now to summarise the conclusions of this chapter. Firstly, the New Testament polemic against Judaism does not allow the concept of natural birth into the covenant people of Israel to be carried over into the New Testament doctrine of the Church. Thus, the infant seed of believers are not to be accounted as members of the visible church on the ground of their birth connection with Christian parents.[18] Secondly, our Lord's teaching does not warrant the popular belief that children, as children, inherit the kingdom of God, but only children who come in faith to him.

Thirdly, the rest of the New Testament is in harmony with the two foregoing conclusions. The practical outworking of these conclusions must be left for consideration in our next chapter.

NOTES

1. J. Munro Gibson, *The Gospel of St. Matthew,* Expositor's Bible series, p. 273.
2. R. V. G. Tasker, *The Gospel According to St. Matthew,* Tyndale New Testament Commentaries series, Tyndale Press, London, 1961, p. 174.
3. *ibid.,* p. 175.
4. See Israel Abrahams, *Studies on Pharisaism and the Gospels,* Vol. 1, p. 41, quoted by B. T. D. Smith, *The Gospel According to St. Matthew,* Cambridge Greek Testament, Cambridge University Press, 1927, p. 162.
5. John E. Meeter (ed.), *Selected Shorter Writings of Benjamin B. Warfield,* Vol. 1, Presbyterian and Reformed, New Jersey, U.S.A., 1970, p. 248.
6. Jewett, *op. cit.,* p. 98.
7. R. E. O. White, "Baptism in the New Testament", in A. Gilmore (ed.), *Christian Baptism,* pp. 105-6, quoted Jewett, *op. cit.,* p. 99.
8. J. Murray, *Christian Baptism,* Presbyterian and Reformed, Philadelphia, 1962, p. 64.
9. G. R. Beasley-Murray, *Baptism in the New Testament,* Macmillan, London, revised edition, 1963, p. 325.
10. *ibid.,* p. 328.
11. Here I am deeply indebted to the argument of my respected mentor, Dr. G. R. Beasley-Murray, *op. cit ,* pp. 324-8.
12. Tasker, *op. cit.,* p. 185.
13. Jewett, *op. cit.,* p. 88.
14. Quoted Jewett, *op. cit.,* p. 88.
15. H. Alford, *Greek Testament,* Rivingtons, London, 1859, in loco., quoted Jewett, *op. cit.,* pp. 221-2.
16. H. Bushnell, *Christian Nurture,* pp. 129-30, quoted Jewett, *op. cit.,* p. 227.
17. In the two preceding paragraphs I largely follow G. R. Beasley-Murray, *op. cit.,* p. 192 ff.
18. A tension is often to be noted in Paedobaptist apologetic. On the one hand it asserts the covenant principle, and so (in theory at least) restricts infant baptism to the children of believers. On the other hand it argues that "if a little child is fit to be a member of the Church in heaven, he is fit to become a member of the Church on earth" (Colquhoun, p. 5). Colquhoun quotes Griffith Thomas with approval, "Surely the truth is that *all* children are included in the great atoning sacrifice, and belong to Jesus Christ until they deliberately refuse him. This is a great spiritual fact at the root of the practice of infant baptism. It is our testimony to the belief that childhood belongs to Christ and has its share in the great redemption. We baptise a child not in order to make it Christ's but because it already belongs to him by the purchase of his sacrifice on Calvary". (W. H. Griffith Thomas, *Principles of Theology,* Church Book Room Press, Canada, fourth edition, 1951, p. 378 (my italics).
If all children are included in the sacrifice of Christ then all children should be baptised. Thomas has provided a theological argument for indiscriminate infant baptism, thereby making the covenant principle irrelevant, yet Colquhoun still maintains it! He does not appear to realise the existence of the tension he has set up. (See his third chapter.)

CHAPTER 7

CHILDREN AND REGENERATION

The subject of children and regeneration is perhaps one of the most difficult which can be considered in the realm of biblical theology. It is difficult for several reasons.

Firstly, there is the paucity of biblical teaching on the subject itself. We have hints and allusions, but nowhere do we find a treatment which could be compared with, for example, the attention given to the subject of justification.

Secondly, there is the problem of relating the mysterious work of regeneration in children (assuming that children can be regenerated) to the expression or manifestation of regeneration in repentance toward God and faith in our Lord Jesus Christ. Can the act of regeneration be separated from its manifestation by a considerable period of time, as some Reformed theologians assume, or are regeneration and its manifestation, though separable in thought, virtually coincidental?

Thirdly, there is the difficulty of relating the demand for repentance and faith, which presupposes intelligent response to the Gospel, to the fact that young children are incapable of making that response.

Fourthly, there is the problem of how the doctrine of original sin and personal accountability before God are to be related to each other. As you will appreciate, every one of these problems bristles with difficulties, and I do not claim to have been able to arrive at nice, neat solutions to all of them.

(i) *Children and their Adamic Status*

We must begin by asserting that the teaching of the New Testament makes it abundantly clear that all men without exception are born in union with Adam into this world. There are two humanities, the old, Adamic humanity and the new humanity in Christ. By birth we are all in the former, but only by re-birth can we enter the latter. In union with Adam all die, for in him all sinned (Rom. 5: 12); in "union" with Christ all are made alive (1 Cor. 15: 22).

To maintain that children are not born in Adam, and thus are not subject from birth to condemnation and death, is to deny the plain teaching of Scripture. Birth connection with Christian parents does not, and cannot, translate a child from union with Adam into union with Christ. Nor is the child to be considered as not being in Adam on the grounds of its supposed innocence until it reaches the age of discretion. Every child of man is born into the Adamic race. If there were exceptions to this rule, it would follow that death has passed not on all, but only on some (Rom. 5: 12).

At this point William B. Coble exposes the problem of trying to maintain an Augustinian doctrine of original sin, on the one hand, and the idea of the innocence of infants on the other. "If we say that a child is innocent or is safe (*not* saved) until he reaches that age at which he becomes accountable to God for the choices which he makes, we do not accept the doctrine of original sin in its true meaning."[1] Rather we must maintain the truth that since every child is born into the Adamic humanity, every child must, if it is to know salvation, be regenerated and transferred into the new humanity in Christ. Children no less than adults require to be regenerated.

The necessity of regeneration in children is demonstrated by two main passages. Firstly, John 3: 6. The contrast drawn throughout the passage between being born and being born again (or from above) proves the point. Whatever the relationship between depravity of nature and the responsible actions of a child may be, at and beyond the point at which accountability is to be reckoned, the implication of John 3: 6 is clear: to be born is to be born of the flesh (*ek tēs sarkos*, cf. John 1: 13 *ek thelēmatos sarkos*). If the meaning of the text is to be upheld it allows of no exceptions—to be born is to be born of the flesh, and thus to be laid under the necessity of being born again in order to see (*i.e.* experience) the kingdom of God (v. 3).

Secondly, 1 Cor. 15: 50. Again, as in Rom. 5, Paul is thinking in terms of the two basic solidarities into which mankind is divided, the Adamic and the Christian (v. 22). The immediate context is, of course, glorification. In verse 50 Paul writes that "flesh and blood cannot inherit the kingdom of God; neither doth corruption inherit incorruption". There must, therefore, be that radical transformation that is termed glorification. But this, though it is the final act of God in the application of redemption, presupposes prior regeneration, for only those who are in union with Christ by faith shall enter into the eternal kingdom of God's glory.

It is hard to see that Paul's language in 1 Cor. 15 admits of the exception of children. Nowhere does he hint that his meaning is to be restricted to responsible adults. Children do not become depraved in Adam when they assume responsibility. Since they are born in Adam they are depraved, by nature, from the very beginning of their existence. If so, they must needs be regenerated by the sovereign power of our gracious God.

We have so far demonstrated that children require to be regenerated no less than adults. We must now consider the ground on which they are regenerated.

(ii) *Children and the Grace of God*

If children require to be regenerated, it must follow, it seems to me, that the ground on which they are regenerated cannot be different from that on which an adult is regenerated.

Needless to say many deny this. Some aver that a child is saved on the ground of its innocence, but this position is false. Firstly, biblically speaking there is no such person as an innocent child, for every child is depraved by nature. Secondly, the concept of innocence cannot be maintained without denying the *grace* of God. If a child is saved on the ground of its innocence then it is not saved by the free and sovereign grace of God. The cause of salvation no longer lies in God alone, but in the child, whom God must save because of its innocence. Clearly grace is no longer grace if such reasoning is accepted.

We must, therefore, insist that a child is saved on just the same basis as an adult, through the sovereign, powerful and efficacious grace of God. We must ever maintain that unless God saves children by free grace they are and will be eternally lost. To state this, of course, does not decide the vexed question of the salvation of children dying in infancy. All children dying in infancy may, for all we know, be saved, but we must insist that if they are it will be only because God is gracious. To maintain otherwise is to pollute the fountain of grace with the corrupt inventions of man's mind.

When one thinks the position through one sees that the situation could not be otherwise. To maintain that a child is safe until it reaches the age of discretion, as many do, is to clutch at a broken reed. Firstly, the Bible nowhere defines an age of discretion. The

94

variety of ages suggested at various times indicates that there is nothing precise on the subject. Secondly, if the age of discretion had been defined, a child dying even one day after that age had been reached without believing in Christ would be lost, whereas had it died two days previously it would have been saved. Surely such reasoning not only lacks a biblical basis, but is positively terrifying in its tying of God to a quite arbitrary date.

If, on the other hand, we maintain that children are saved by grace alone we have true hope. The ground of our hope is not in the supposed innocence of children but in the grace and mercy of the God and Father of our Lord Jesus Christ. True, children are born with depraved natures, but equally true is the fact that such natures have never been able, ultimately, to resist the overtures of grace when God purposes to save his elect.

We still face the fact that in the New Testament the receiving of salvation is conditional upon the response of believing faith. (I am assuming that this response is itself wrought by God, although at the same time it is a truly human and personal response.) Yet children, or more precisely, small children, are held to be psychologically incapable of receiving the truths of the Gospel into their minds and believing unto salvation.

So much stress is placed upon the young child's psychological incapacity to believe (presumably with the desire to maintain the child's supposed innocence) that the position is reached that God can save in the full New Testament sense of the word only if the age of psychological capacity has been reached. But again grace is denied to be grace and we are plunged into difficulty.

If the Scriptures define neither the age of discretion nor the age of psychological capacity to believe, when are these reached? How may this turning point be recognised? What of adult imbeciles? Are they beyond the grace of God because of psychological incapacity? Surely not!

One accepts, of course, that a young child's understanding of the Gospel may be very simple when compared with that of an adult, but there are too many recorded instances of very young children believing the Gospel in a very clear fashion for us to suppose that alleged psychological incapacity continues for many years.[2] When one reads such statements as the following from a recent Southern Baptist publication one can only gasp in amazement. "The New Testament vocabulary of sin represents acts which are essentially adult in nature. The vast majority of the words are utterly meaningless to the *pre-teen* children."³ These words illustrate the danger of the notion of psychological incapacity. What parent, failing to see the signs of conversion, would not desire to extend the period of alleged incapacity into the teens? But how unsatisfactory such a notion is.

There is a deeper reason why the idea of psychological incapacity is unsatisfactory and it is this: it suggests that God cannot save a child until that child is psychologically ready for faith. The consequence is that there are two types of salvation, the salvation of those dying in infancy and the salvation of those surviving infancy to reach the age of psychological capacity for faith. The former salvation is available, it would appear, because the infant is both innocent and psychologically incapable of exercising faith, the latter because the age of sufficient maturity has been reached.

In opposition to this we cannot too strenuously insist that there is but one salvation. We must also insist, in the light of New Testament theology, that psychological incapacity is no barrier to the operation of God's Spirit in saving power in infants. Those who make so much of the psychological incapacity of children seem to forget the psychological incapacity of adults. Yet Scripture is emphatic as to its existence, and insistent that it can be overcome only as God recreates a man through regeneration. But "the natural man receiveth not the things of the Spirit of God: for they are foolishness unto him: neither can he know them, because they are spiritually discerned" (1 Cor. 2: 14). "But if our gospel be hid, it is hid to them that are lost: In whom the god of this world hath blinded the minds of them which believe not, lest the light of the glorious gospel of Christ, who is the image of God, should shine unto them" (2 Cor. 4: 3, 4). If this type of constitutional psychological inability to believe is no barrier to God's grace, why should the psychological inability of infants prevent the operation of divine grace?

We must, it seems to me, strenuously maintain that God is able to regenerate infants by free and sovereign grace. We may not be able to understand how the apparent lack of understanding in very young children relates to the New Testament requirement of a measure of intelligent assent to the Gospel. However, we dare not make our inability to understand the ground for denying that God can and does work in whom he will. We must affirm that no unregenerate person is able to enter into the kingdom of God, and so infants and children must be regenerated in order to enjoy the bliss of heaven, but we dare not maintain that God cannot regenerate a child from its earliest infancy. If he can fill some with the Holy Spirit from their mother's womb,[4] he can certainly regenerate in infancy, whether or not we can understand how this comes to pass or how it has its outworking.

It is important to be clear that faith is never to be regarded as a merit by which we are saved. Faith is the instrument of salvation which joins us to Christ. We are not saved *on account of* our faith (*dia pistiv*) but *through* faith (*dia pisteōs* or *ek pisteōs*). Therefore, God will not refuse to save infants on the ground of their incapacity for faith, nor on the other hand will he save them on the ground of their innocence. Grace, and grace alone, is the cause of our salvation. Faith is the instrument by which we appropriate the blessings of the Gospel, but it is not the meritorious cause of our salvation. This being the case, our emphasis must be upon God's grace (his willingness) and power (his ability) to save children. Rather than emphasising the incapacity of children we must proclaim the capacity of God. In other words, we must place our emphasis upon the power of God through his Spirit to save children. This is what the authors of the Westminster Confession do: "elect infants, dying in infancy, are regenerated and saved by Christ through the Spirit, who worketh when, and where, and how he pleaseth". Nothing is impossible with God.

(iii) *Infant salvation*

It is popularly supposed that all infants dying in infancy are saved. Many reformed divines have extended the phrase "elect infants" to mean that all infants dying in infancy are elect, although it is questionable whether such a thought was in the minds of the authors of the Westminster Confession. Some, like Spurgeon, have maintained that heaven will contain more infants than adults, since the greater proportion of the human race has probably died in infancy.

It seems to me that if Spurgeon, Hodge and Boettner do not intentionally go beyond Scripture, they certainly take the barest hints and press them so much that they become the assertion of this doctrine of infant salvation. But nowhere in Scripture, as far as I can see, is there express warrant for this belief.

This is not to say that God cannot save all children dying in infancy, nor to say that he does not, it is simply to recognise the fact that he has not chosen to tell us whether he does or not.

As we have seen in previous chapters, there is no ground for supposing that being born of believing parents entitles one to baptism, yet this is just the ground on which many Paedobaptists argue for the regeneration of infants. Since the ground on which a covenant child is to be baptised is presumptive regeneration, should that child die in infancy it is to be assumed to have been regenerated. James Buchanan advances this as his main argument.[5]

Scripture itself indicates, however, that being born of believing parents is not a ground for baptising infants, therefore it is not a ground for presuming that children of Christian parents who die in infancy are to be adjudged regenerate. If one upholds the practice of infant baptism on the ground of covenant theology and at the same time holds that all children dying in infancy are saved (as Hodge and Boettner do) then one faces another problem. Children of unbelieving parents who die in infancy must be presumed regenerate on some other ground than connection by birth, with resultant interest in the covenant. If it is that *as children* they are precious to the Saviour and are the subjects of his redemptive work, then there is no need to appeal to birth connection in the case of children of believing parents who die in infancy. The general includes the particular.

My own position is that in the matter of infant salvation one can only adopt an attitude of reverent and hopeful agnosticism.[6] One dare not add to Scripture, but neither must one make the deduction from Scripture that God cannot or will not save all children dying in infancy. The salvation of all children dying in infancy is not asserted in Scripture, nor is the condemnation of such children asserted. The mercy of our God is free and large. That we know.

Yet if we are consistent Calvinists we can be no more certain of the election of our children than of the children of unbelievers.[7] John Tombes, another Calvinistic Baptist of the 17th century was more optimistic, believing that even as God's love had been revealed in the election of the parents so it would be revealed in the election of infants, but "to make God consider (as the object of childen's election) the faith of their parents, is worse than the opinion of the

Arminians who make faith and works foreseen the object of every particular man's election . . .".[8]

In the end we are brought to rest in the mystery of election. Salvation depends upon God's election and not upon parentage. "The elect are known only to God, but because they are his through free grace and not for the faith of their fathers, there can be no limit set to God's election."[9]

(iv) *Children and church membership*

Finally, a brief word about the church relationship of the children of believers. It is true that birth connection does not entitle them to church membership, but it is also true that such connection is brought about by God in his providence so that they, as John Tombes says, are "born in the bosom of the church, of godly parents, who by prayers, instruction, example, will undoubtedly educate them in the true faith of Christ . . .".[10] This, however, is one thing; to regard their privilege as evidence of their status as *Christian* children is another. Believers' children are privileged children because they are within the sphere of the preaching and nurture of the church, but they are not made Christian children by privilege, but by true conversion. We dare not confuse privilege with position or status. Our children are born into the Adamic race and we dare not presume that they have been regenerated until they give real evidence of the saving change.

This is where our view of children in relation to the church is of vital, practical importance. We treat our children as if they were unconverted until we are satisfied that they are; Paedobaptists if they are consistent treat them as converted, Christian children. For example, in his recent book *Evangelism in the Early Church* E. M. B. Green has this to say:

> "In none of these instances (referring to evidence of the presence of children in the New Testament church) is there any suggestion that direct evangelising is necessary or fitting in a Christian house. Indeed, the children of believers are already treated as being in the Christian fellowship unless they contract out; like the child of a proselyte to Judaism they are regarded as within the covenant unless they determine to cut themselves off from it. And even then they do not need to be converted in the sense which we examine in Chapter 6; rather they need to be corrected by

their parents and brought back to the Christian way from which they had strayed."[11]

Only one comment is necessary. To one such covenant child, now adult, and still contracted in, our Lord said, with not one "verily" but two, "Ye must be born again".[12] If we do not teach and impress upon our children *that* necessity, we shall fail them at the very point of their deepest need.

NOTES

1. In Clifford Ingle (ed.), *Children and Conversion*, pp. 59-60, Broadman Press, Nashville, U.S.A., 1970.
2. See *e.g.* Jonathan Edwards' account of the conversion of Phebe Bartlet, aged four years, in "A Narrative of Surprising Conversions", *The Select Works of Jonathan Edwards*, Vol. 1, Banner of Truth Trust, London, pp. 109-13.
3. William B. Coble in Clifford Ingle (ed.), *op. cit.*, p. 61.
4. Luke 1: 15.
5. James Buchanan, *The Office and Work of the Holy Spirit*, Banner of Truth Trust edition, London, 1966, chap. 8.
6. Agnosticism in the sense of not knowing because of lack of clear scriptural data, not in the philosophical sense that the existence of anything beyond the material world cannot be known.
7. John Tombes, *Examen of the Sermon of Mr. Stephen Marshall about Infant Baptism, London,* 1645, p. 32, quoted Walker, *op. cit.*, p. 256.
8. Henry Lawrence, *Of Baptism* (1646), pp. 149-50, quoted Walker, *op. cit.*, p. 256.
9. Walker, op. cit., p. 260.
10. John Tombes, *Examen*, p. 33, quoted Walker, *op. cit.*, p. 256.
11. E. M. B. Green, *Evangelism in the Early Church*, Hodder & Stoughton, London, 1970, p. 220.
12. John 3: 3.

INDEX

ACCOUNTABILITY, Age of, 70, 72-3, 94-5
Adam, 9, 63, 92-4
Alexander, Dr. J. W., 63
Alford, H., 88, 91
Anabaptists, 13, 19, 23, 30, 64
Andrews, Jedediah, 63-4
Angels, 82, 84
Anglo-Catholicism, 18

BANNER OF TRUTH, 37, 58, 66
Bannerman, Douglas, 41, 48
— James, 28, 37, 57-8, 65, 66, 67
Baptist Quarterly, 77
Baptist Union of Great Britain and Ireland, 21, 22, 77
Baptists, non-Reformed (Arminian), 17-18, 55, 56, 68
— Reformed (Calvinistic), 5, 7, 13, 18, 19-20, 23, 55-6, 57, 59-62, 67, 68, 98
Barth, Karl, 5, 25, 36
Beasley-Murray, G. R., 37, 66, 77, 85, 87, 91
Bird, Herbert, 42-3
Black, Constance, 14
Boettner, L., 48, 97, 98
Booth, Abraham, 18, 55, 56
Border Baptist Association, 14
Buchanan, James, 98, 100
Bunyan, John, 18
Bushnell, H., 91
Buswell, J. O., Jr., 37

CALVIN, John, 30-1, 46, 47, 66
Canaan, 6, 30, 32, 39, 50, 51, 65
Carey Conference 14
Carson, Alexander, 18
— Herbert M., 14, 66
Children, theology of, 5, 8, 9, 14, 21, 68, 73-4
Church, doctrine of, 57-60, 90
— membership of, 7, 10, 13, 37, 43, 47, 57-62, 76, 81, 91, 99
Circumcision and baptism, 5-6, 17, 22, 23-35, 40-2, 45, 55, 60, 71
— in the New Testament, 33-5, 53-4
— institution and observance of, 29, 44, 46, 68, 69

Circumcision, significance of, 6, 8, 17, 26-8, 31, 39, 42, 45, 50, 53-4
Clark, Neville, 77
Clements, R. E., 72, 77
Coble, William B., 93, 100
Colquhoun, Frank, 40, 48, 91
Confession of Faith, Baptist, of 1667 and 1689, 7, 59-60
——— *Westminster*, 59, 97
Covenant, Abrahamic, 6, 7, 17, 24-5, 27-33, 38-9, 44-5, 56, 57, 65, 68
— blessings, 16, 31, 40, 42, 45, 46
— children, 8, 46-7, 62-4, 86, 87, 88, 98
— community, 8, 45, 68-74, 75, 77, 80
— grace, 7, 16, 56
— Mosaic, 17, 28, 75-6
— of grace, 5, 20-2, 23, 38, 61, 66
— sign, 17, 23-4, 25, 27-8, 31-3, 43, 45-6, 53-4, 63, 70
— theology, 5, 14, 15-23, 28, 38-47, 50, 65, 98

DABNEY, R., 64, 66
Dalman, G., 85
Davies, G. Henton, 74, 77
Directory for the Public Worship of God, 46
Donatists, 57

EDWARDS, Jonathan, 60, 66, 100
Election, 8, 56, 67, 74, 76-7, 80, 81

FOUNDATIONS, 77

GIBSON, J. Munro, 80-1, 91
Gill, John, 18
Gilmore, Alec, 77
Gospel Magazine, 39, 48
Green, E. M. B., 99, 100

HARAN, 68-9
Harrelson, W., 77
Heaney, Rev. J. L., 39
Heidelburg Catechism (1563), 23
Hodge, Charles, 8, 37, 47, 64, 65, 67, 76, 77, 97, 98

Hughes, Philip Edgcumbe, 36
Hulse, Erroll, 14

INFANT baptism, 5, 8, 15, 18-19, 21-2,
   23-5, 28, 35-6, 38, 40-1, 47, 48, 55,
   62, 63, 64, 67, 86, 88, 89, 91
— salvation, 10, 63, 96, 97-8
Ingle, Clifford, 77, 100
Irish Baptist College, 14
Isaac, 45, 81
Ishmael, 30, 45-6, 81
Israel, 5, 6, 7, 27, 32, 33, 35, 39, 43, 47,
   55, 57, 61, 68, 69, 72, 74, 76, 81, 89
Israelite 42-3, 69, 71, 72, 73

JEROME, 85
Jewett, Paul K., 20, 22, 29, 31, 33, 37,
   40, 42, 45, 46, 48, 49, 55, 66, 71,
   77, 91
Jonker, Dr. E., 14
Judah, 74, 75
Judaism, 41-2, 69, 79, 84, 89, 90, 99

KLINE, Meredith, 44-5, 48, 49
Kuyper, Dr. Abraham, 62

LAWRENCE, Henry, 100
Legg, Rev. John, 14
Lightfoot, J. B., 52, 66
Lord's Supper, 17, 18, 71
Lutheranism, 18

MACLAREN, Alexander, 66
Marcel, Pierre Charles, 25, 32, 36, 37,
   41
Marcion, 17
Martin, Ralph P., 53, 66
Meeter, John E., 91
Murray, Professor John, 15-16, 22, 24,
   37, 45, 47, 49, 58, 85, 91

NATIONAL Foundation for Christian Education, 22
Noah, 74-5

ORIGEN, 85
Original sin, doctrine of, 73, 83, 93

PAEDOBAPTISTS, 5, 6, 7, 15-16, 21,
   23-4, 28, 35-6, 38-42, 45-7, 48, 50,
   52, 53, 55, 56, 57, 58, 62, 65, 67,
   68, 70, 71, 75, 88, 89, 91, 98

102

Passover, 17, 43, 48, 71, 73
Patient, Thomas, 18
Payne, E. A., 36
Pentecost, 89
Phillips, Anthony, 70, 77
Plummer, A., 85
Pretoria Central Baptist Church, 14
Proselyte baptism, 6, 41, 84
Psychological capacity for belief, 95-6

REFORMATION, 19, 23
Reformers, 18, 23
Regeneration, 6, 9, 13, 19, 29, 34, 54,
   62, 64, 92-4, 96, 98
Remnant, concept of, 8, 74-6
Robinson, H. Wheeler, 75, 77
Roman Catholic doctrine, 5, 18-19, 48
Rowley, H. H., 48
Runia, Klaas, 19
Rusling, G. W., 77

SCHENCK, Lewis Bevins, 62, 63, 64
Schmid, J., 85
Seed, concept and interpretation of, 6,
   7, 16-17, 30, 32-4, 35, 36, 39-40,
   47, 50-5, 60-1, 68, 80-1, 90
Septuagint, 84
Shepard, Thomas, 37
Spurgeon, Charles H., 18, 60, 97

TASKER, R. V. G., 83, 88, 91
Theocracy, 39, 43, 61
Thomas, W. H. Griffith, 91
Thornwell, J. H., 64, 66
Tombes, John, 98, 99, 100
Turretine, Francis, 35

VERDUIN, L., 62, 66

WALKER, M. J., 77, 100
Warfield, B. B., 83, 84, 91
Watson, T. E., 37
Weiss, J., 85
Wells, Dr. Robin, 14
White, R. E. O., 85, 91
Windisch, H., 88
Wright, G. Ernest, 55, 66

YAHWISM, 70
Young, E. J., 35, 37

ZWINGLI, Ulrich, 18-19, 22

INDEX OF SCRIPTURE REFERENCES

David Kingdon is an associate editor of *Reformation Today*, a forty page quarterly published by the Cuckfield Baptist Church, Sussex. Why not write for a free sample copy from Carey Publications? The purpose of the magazine is to stimulate a desire for reformation of doctrine and practice among evangelical churches. The magazine is enjoying an increasing circulation the world over.

In *Preaching Yesterday and Today,* a ninety-six page paperback retailing at 45p, there are five chapters. The first reminds us of the powerful preaching of George Whitefield. The second examines Luther's doctrine of the human will. The third and fourth are by David Kingdon. He writes on the subject, God's Church and Scriptural Evangelism, followed by an analysis of the Secular Society. The implications of Biblical theology for our preaching are considered in the final chapter. Order from Carey or Walter.

Henry E. Walter Ltd. publish a twenty-four page catechism for boys and girls which is ideal for family worship. The price (1973) is 12p. The catechism deals with questions about God, Man and Sin, Salvation, the Ten Commandments, Prayer, the Church, the Ordinances and the Last Things. It is attractively produced. While on the subject of children there is an excellent chapter on the nurture of children in *The Ideal Church* (96 pages, 45p) by Terence Aldridge. In the same volume Ian Tait writes on the subject of Missionary Outreach and the Local Church. A Carey production which can be ordered from Walter or Carey.